The St. Martin's Resource Library in Political Science

BIG IDEAS

An Introduction to Ideologies in American Politics

The St. Martin's Resource Library in Political Science

BIG IDEAS

An Introduction to Ideologies in American Politics

R. Mark Tiller
Houston Community College

St. Martin's Press
New York

Sponsoring editor: Beth A. Gillett
Development editor: Ted Whitten
Managing editor: Patricia Mansfield Phelan
Production supervisor: Kurt Nelson
Art director: Lucy Krikorian
Cover art and photo: Stock Connection © 1996 Joe Sohm / Chromosohm
Composition: Ewing Systems

Manufactured in the United States of America.

1 0 9 8 7
f e d c b a

For information, write:
St. Martin's Press, Inc.
175 Fifth Avenue
New York, NY 10010

ISBN 0-312-15372-4

CONTENTS

PREFACE

Why study ideology? It is hard to imagine another subject as important as ideology. At the individual level, it is at the root of almost everything uniquely human—our dreams, our ethics, our security, our fears, our relationships, and our pursuit of happiness. On a social scale, it is about ideas that change the world.

Nonetheless, ideology is one of the more difficult subjects to teach, for a variety of reasons. Some students initially think ideology is "just theory" and therefore irrelevant to their everyday lives. Many students find ideology a difficult subject because it requires a great deal of critical thought rather than memorization and repetition. Studying ideology may frustrate others because it arouses strong feelings and challenges deeply held convictions. Both students and teachers find it difficult to be entirely objective about a subject that is inherently subjective. Because introductory government or political science textbooks must cover so many topics, they typically devote only one chapter to ideology—there simply isn't enough space in a textbook for a more lengthy discussion. Unfortunately, most books about ideology are too difficult for the average reader and assume a great deal of prior knowledge.

However, these difficulties do not excuse the educator and the student from studying such an important subject. Ideology cannot be avoided in the study of government. Consider how often terms like *liberal, elitist, authoritarian, communist, democrat,* and *nationalist* are used in the press and elsewhere. In fact, quite often the terms are misused and mean different things to different people. This alone is reason enough to study ideology more carefully so that we may share a common vocabulary and enjoy a more meaningful discussion. *Big Ideas: An Introduction to Ideologies in American Politics* is an attempt to overcome some of these challenges. With it, I hope to help bridge the gap between scholarly works on ideology and political science textbooks.

Ideology is a complex subject with its own vocabulary. It is not an irrelevant subject of eighteenth-century writers. Great philosophical debates, which are critical to our lives today, are still raging among intellectuals. The conclusions they reach are shaped by the accumulated ideological thought of past centuries. These conclusions shape our modern world, determining policies about issues such as gun control, taxation, privacy rights, and so on. Indeed, modern political battles are rooted in a history of ideological debate. Unfortunately, such debates are largely incomprehensible to most of us. The primary goal of this text is to give the student a window into this important subject. I have tried to write it in common English and have assumed little prior knowledge of ideology. Of course, readers who are already well versed in the subject may find it overly simplistic.

TO THE INSTRUCTOR

Educational texts about ideology are typically organized historically, beginning with the classical Mediterranean or seventeenth-century European ideology. Although this approach has an obvious appeal, too often students become overwhelmed with concepts and unfamiliar terms about an era that is obscure to their experiences. This text instead begins with the ideological concepts that are most important to the study of contemporary American politics (liberal and conservative). Part One is organized thematically, or conceptually; it defines the social, political, and economic ideological concepts that will be used in the second part of the text. Part Two is a historically ordered discussion of the great ideological movements of the last three hundred years.

For nine years, I have used a previous version of this text as a supplement to traditional political science texts in my introductory government course. I find it most useful when it is married to a beginning unit on the U.S. Constitution. My students read Part One first, Chapters 6 and 7 while studying the Constitution, and the remainder of the text after studying the Constitution. This approach helps the students appreciate that the Constitution was not written in a vacuum, and it allows them to compare the American constitutional system to the values and experiences of other countries. This text has also been used in comparative politics courses.

TO THE STUDENT

The organization of this text may seem odd to some readers, because frequently it returns to ideas or themes discussed in previous chapters. Occasionally it also briefly mentions something to come in a later chapter. Such disorder is to some degree inescapable, because to fully understand one ideological concept it is necessary to understand others. This presents the dilemma of where to begin. Therefore the reader is encouraged to look backward as needed. Throughout the reading, there are names of famous ideological thinkers, dates, historical examples, statistics, and so on. These are not unimportant, but they are provided primarily to aid in your comprehension of ideology. It is my opinion that study of the ideological concepts themselves is much more useful than memorization of the examples and names associated with them.

Each chapter ends with a few key terms and study questions. These terms and questions are not the only ideas of importance in the chapter. However, they can serve as a good test of your comprehension. You may wish to write essay-form answers in response to the study questions. As for the key terms, define them in your own words without copying from the text or a dictionary. If you cannot explain them in your own words, you probably need to study them again. Also, don't stop with a simple definition: explain the relevance of each term. Discuss how each relates to other terms and concepts. Give examples. Note the origins of the terms. This kind of study will give you a superior understanding of ideology.

CONCLUSION

Some people believe that the participation of the people in politics is critical to the well-being of our country. One commonly hears the assertion: "We need to get the people involved in the process. If only the people became more informed and assertive . . . if only they voted . . . if only they demanded good government of their representatives."

Others consider the apathy of the mass public to be a blessing. They argue that the majority of the public will never educate themselves enough to make a constructive contribution. In this view, many of our problems are caused precisely because politicians try too hard to cater to the unwise and selfish demands of those who become marginally politically active.

Both of these positions have some merit. My own opinion is that if the public is going to participate in political debates, it is incumbent on educators and students to do everything we can to make that participation meaningful. If we are going to insist on democracy, we should at least know what democracy means!

ACKNOWLEDGMENTS

I would like to thank Neal Tannahill, Southwest College dean of instructional services for Houston Community College System (HCCS), for reviewing my rough draft. Thanks also to HCCS instructors Hal Comello, Dale Foster, Mary Frazier, Michelle Gagnier, Mark Hartray, Steven McAleavy, and Lee McGriggs, and to journalist Jermaine Nkrumah, for their helpful comments. Finally, the most important advice has come from my many students who took the time to explain to me what they did and did not understand about ideology. They are both my audience and co-authors.

R. Mark Tiller

PART ONE
Ideologies

There are literally hundreds of words that distinguish variations of ideological thought, many of which overlap. To complicate matters even more, there are many interpretations for each ideology. Fierce arguments rage between philosophers (even of the same ideology) over the true meaning of their ideology. Part One tries to unravel each of the basic ideological terms.

In Chapter 1, the concept of *ideology* itself is discussed. Chapter 2 explains the modern-day usage of the terms *liberalism* and *conservatism* (and *left* and *right*) in great detail. These terms are probably the most important ideological concepts.

The left-to-right spectrum is one way by which ideological concepts can be classified. Another is by subject. Most ideologies are *primarily* concerned with one of three subjects:

- social systems (how people relate to each other)
- political systems (the power relationship between the people and their government)
- economic systems (the control of wealth, property, and production).

These issues overlap, so it is quite arbitrary to divide them; but in the interest of simplification they are herein treated separately in Chapters 3, 4, and 5, concerning (respectively) *social ideologies, political ideologies*, and *economic ideologies*.

CHAPTER 1

WHAT IS IDEOLOGY?

The root of the term **ideology** comes from the Greek word *ide*, which means "idea" or "image." In modern usage ideology is a system of ideas, or a vision, of how life should be organized—socially, politically, and economically. One might also include religious ideology in this classification scheme, although this is not our topic. In fact, philosophers began to commonly use the term *ideology* during the French Revolution to refer to the revolutionaries' view (as opposed to the Catholic Church's view) of how society should be organized.

To repeat, ideology is a *system* of ideas—not just random, disassociated thoughts but a complex, or web, of interlocking ideas, concepts, theories, and perceptions. These ideas support and add to one another. Ideologies are not right or wrong; they cannot be proved or disproved. Taken as a whole, an ideology presents a powerful logical and/or emotional argument for a particular course of action. Individuals who are attracted to an ideology are called **ideologues**. Although the term *ideologue* has a somewhat negative connotation in the United States today, it simply means a person who believes in and is motivated by ideology.

Ideologies have many functions. They provide standards by which people can evaluate right and wrong. They also may be considered as theories, for predictive purposes. Ideologues think that ideology explains the past, helps them understand the present, and allows them to anticipate what will come in the future. In addition, ideologies may be used

3

to consider ideals and help people set goals toward reaching those ideals. More actively, ideologies often suggest methods that are appropriate to meet such goals, and solutions to perceived problems. Finally, ideologies provide a rallying call to action, which organizes people into groups—by which participants define themselves and judge who is an enemy and who is a friend. For some ideologues, ideology becomes a critical part of their identity. This explains why it is so difficult for such people to critically examine their own values and consider new ones.

Ideologies may also be used by political leaders and others to propagandize and manipulate people. In such cases, ideology may be employed as a facade to cloak the political ambitions of individuals or groups. Through ideological control of education, government, business, culture, and so on, rulers control the agenda and make alternatives to their policies simply unthinkable. By indoctrinating the public with the "correct" way to think, they stifle opposition and serious debate. Such ideological policing is easy to spot in undemocratic countries. Yet, Americans are also subject to this phenomenon, although it occurs in much more subtle forms.

All people—including Americans—undergo **political socialization**, that is, the process by which political views are acquired. This process of lifelong learning (and relearning) helps determine which ideologies attract our attention. It begins during childhood, as parents and school-teachers teach reverence for patriotic historical events, myths, and symbols and tell idealistic stories of heroic leaders and role models. It continues via friends and peer groups such as interest groups, political parties, and churches. In the current information age, the media plays an increasingly large role in socialization. Of course, as the previous paragraph implies, this political socialization can be heavily controlled by political leaders in pursuit of their own agendas, through the use of ideological propaganda via the media. The power of the American media to promote ideological values through symbolism and entertainment is especially great, although it is not focused in a single ideological direction or for a particular purpose as in countries with controlled sources of information. Ideological constraints on public policy making in the United States may be just as effective, but they are not imposed conspiratorially by a ruling class.

It should be noted that leaders, too, are bound by their people's dominant ideological values. Ideas that have been previously condemned as alien are ruled out before they can even be considered. In fact, even when a new proposal is *not* ideologically alien to a country, its opponents generally try to portray it as such. Political victories often depend on which side successfully frames the issue in terms of the dominant ideologies of the country.

Consider the debate over health-care reform. As President Clinton's health-care reform proposal neared completion in late 1993, proponents of universal coverage (health insurance for all) tried to portray the issue in terms of *equality and fairness*. Former senator Harris Wofford (D-Pennsylvania) suggested, "If all criminals are guaranteed the right to lawyers, then certainly all citizens deserve a right to doctors." Opponents of universal coverage labeled the Clinton health-care plan *socialist*. They tried instead to focus attention on the role of government in the plan and the tax burden on private businesses. Of course, in the United States equality and fairness are positive ideological values, whereas socialism and taxation are negative. The adoption or rejection of Clinton's plan probably depended most on which ideological framework was more popularly accepted by the people and their representatives. Objectively, one could take issue with each of the arguments: all Americans already get health care, because if they do not have insurance they will be admitted for treatment in publicly-owned hospital emergency rooms or charity clinics. The real issue is whether this is the most cost-efficient manner by which to provide that service. Furthermore, as former senator Bob Dole (R-Kansas) pointed out, the overwhelming majority of Americans already consider their health care to be the best in the world. As for "socialism" and taxation, the government's role in the Clinton plan was minimal in comparison to that of most of our allies' health-care systems, as well as in comparison plans offered by congressional liberals. Americans already pay for the burden of indigent health care at the state and local level, so the primary effect would have been to redistribute the tax burden rather than increase it. If successful, reform could even reduce the cost of health care. However, such arguments probably had less to do with the ultimate failure of the Clinton plan than did the success of his opponents in controlling the ideological debate. After all, ideological values are much easier to evaluate than complicated arguments about tax rates and pharmaceutical regulations, since most citizens already possess opinions about ideology, for better or worse.

In 1995, Clinton was able to turn the ideological tables regarding Medicare, a health insurance entitlement for Social Security beneficiaries. The newly elected Republican majority in Congress proposed a seven-year plan to cut $270 billion from the projected costs of Medicare. By pointing out that the Republicans also proposed a $245 billion tax cut that would disproportionately benefit the wealthy, Clinton was able to resurrect the theme of equality and fairness. The Republicans insisted that their tax cuts would be paid for by other reductions in spending, and that under their plan, the average annual spending per Medicare recipient would rise from $4,800 to $6,700. They took opinion polls and held strategy sessions to debate alternative words to be used instead of *cut*, finally settling on *improve, protect,* and *preserve* (Medicare). Clinton and congressional Democrats noted that in order to provide merely the current level of services, Medicare spending would have to rise to $8,000 per recipient, owing to the high inflation rate of medical costs; therefore the Republican plan was clearly a *cut*—moreover, a cut from vulnerable Medicare recipients "to pay for a tax break for the wealthy." This argument resonates with Americans' ideological preference for fairness and equality.

As the new Congress met in early 1997, there was no agreement on how Medicare costs should be controlled, although politicians of all stripes agree that it must be somehow restructured, generally through encouragement of managed care and health maintenance organizations. (Compared to the contentious debate over Social Security and Medicaid, there is great consensus in principle.) In fact, both sides agree that much of the Medicare savings should come at the expense of wealthy Medicare beneficiaries, who would be required to pay higher premiums. In early 1996, the Republicans lowered their proposed cuts to $168 billion, much closer to the president's proposal of $118 billion. So why did the public mistrust the congressional Republicans' effort to "improve, protect, and preserve" Medicare? It probably is *not* because the public had a clear understanding of the difference between the president's and the Republicans' proposals, and how each would reform Medicare spending. The public understood the Medicare debate no more than it understood the debate about Clinton's health insurance proposal. Rather, the mistrust was more likely owing to the powerful ideological appeal of the president's argument for fairness and equality. The Republicans had arguments to support their proposals, but not much of an ideological basis from which to present them.

The preceding discussion is not meant to suggest that the American public is consciously ideological. In fact, rather than seeking ideologues to govern them, most Americans say they prefer nonideological approaches to government. Yet the devotion of Republicans for Ronald Reagan and the devotion of Democrats for Franklin Roosevelt and John Kennedy suggests otherwise. Although these men were controversial figures, no one can doubt the strength of their leadership and vision. Ideologues believe that a solid ideological foundation is essential to great leadership and decision making. For a president—who must translate complex ideas to the mass public, and whose success often depends on his ability to rally and motivate the public—ideology is indispensable.

"It is easy to build a philosophy—it doesn't have to run."
—Charles Kettering

Those who are less ideological often label themselves **problem-solvers** or **pragmatists**, implying they are more practical than theoretical. Problem-solvers accuse ideologues of being wedded to their defunct theories and failed methods of the past. They purport to be free of ideological restraints and blinders; they tend to emphasize "practical methods" and "whatever works." After all, they claim, the world's most influential ideologies today originated hundreds of years ago, in very different societies with very different problems. Compared to Ronald Reagan, both George Bush and Bill Clinton are problem-solvers. They have devoted their lives to public service and policy study. Both are arguably harder working and more intellectually capable than Reagan was. However, their support has been shallow and relatively unenthusiastic. Bush's lack of appreciation for the continual questions about his long-term goals and values became evident when in a moment of frustration he awkwardly referred to the issue as "the vision thing." Likewise Clinton, who calls himself a "New Democrat" (implying a willingness to rethink his party's ideology), is continually accused of waffling on the issues and standing for nothing. Both men have been accused by their own supporters of compromising too much.

> "When you don't know where you're going, any gust of wind will get you there."
>
> —Unknown

Ideologues argue that many ideological controversies are not specific to a particular time—that many questions put forth by philosophers two thousand years ago are just as relevant today. Furthermore, those who have no ideological perspective to guide themselves have a haphazard or random way of understanding what should and should not be changed, and they usually make short-term "Band-Aid" solutions to long-term problems.

Still others believe that both sides in the preceding argument are correct. Ideology *is* indispensable to politics, they argue. However, all societies should constantly reevaluate their intellectual foundations, revising outdated and counterproductive ideologies when appropriate. According to this line of thinking, because societies are made up of individual people, individuals must be open-minded enough to reconsider their ideological values. This is especially important in light of the fact that the ideological positions themselves are not frozen in time and place. Ideology and ideologues are not static but dynamic—frequently changing and adapting to the present environment because of dramatic events, controversial issues, political campaigns, popular leaders, and a variety of other socializing influences.

Key Terms

ideology
ideologue
political socialization
problem-solver/pragmatist

Study Questions

1. What is ideology?
2. What positive social purpose does ideology serve? How is ideology abused?
3. What are the advantages and disadvantages of ideologues and problem-solvers as leaders?

CHAPTER 2

IDEOLOGY IN AMERICAN POLITICS

LIBERALISM AND CONSERVATISM

One cannot understand politics without understanding ideology. In the United States, ideology is expressed in the mainstream media most often through the debate between *conservatives* and *liberals*. Each of these terms has both a classical (original) meaning and a modern meaning. The classical liberals were European (and to a lesser degree, American) philosophers, primarily of the seventeenth and eighteenth centuries. They advocated constitutionalism, free enterprise capitalism, religious freedom, individualism, civil liberty, and an end to feudalism. Social scientists today refer to their ideology as **classical liberalism**. This philosophy acted as the intellectual basis of the American revolutionaries and constitutional framers. Classical liberalism is the subject of Chapter 6.

The primary opponents of the classical liberals were the European aristocracies and the system of feudal monarchism that the liberals directly challenged. However, there was also an intellectual opposition to the liberals, which social scientists call **classical conservatism**. Both the conservatives and liberals were a part of the same great philosophical movement that we refer to today as the *Enlightenment*. However, the conservatives believed the pace and scope of the radical changes advocated by the liberals was too great. Classical conservatism is discussed in Chapter 7.

The classical meanings of these terms have been largely forgotten in the United States. This is partly because the classical debate between liberals and conservatives took place chiefly among Europeans, not among Americans. Classical liberalism was much more influential in the United States, where classical conservatism had few advocates. Modern American liberals are the descendants of classical liberalism, although they have redefined many of liberalism's ideas and have reformed it with the addition of new principles. Modern American conservatism is also primarily a product of classical liberalism, although it has retained many of classical conservatism's tenets as well. The evolution of each term will be more easily appreciated after reading Chapters 6 and 7.

MODERN AMERICAN LIBERALISM AND CONSERVATISM

The modern debate between American liberals and conservatives is essentially a dispute concerning the government's role in promoting progressive change in society. **Liberals** generally favor changes, or reforms. They tend to believe in *positive* government—that government can and should help promote social progress. They advocate a relatively active role for the government in promoting social justice, political equality, and economic prosperity. **Conservatives** are more reluctant to endorse change and tend to favor the status quo (the existing condition). They emphasize the positive aspects of the present system and want to *conserve* what is good. Conservatives often do not agree with liberals' definitions of what is wrong and in need of correction. Alternatively, they simply may be suspicious of attempts to reform the status quo—they fear that with the attempt to correct relatively minor problems of the present, reformers will sacrifice the benefits of the status quo as well. Conservatives are not opposed to change in principle but often believe that liberal reforms are too radical. In this sense, their opposition to liberalism is comparable to the classical conservatives' critique of classical liberalism. In both cases, conservatives have argued that the pace of change is too great.

Ironically, both liberals and conservatives are critical of government in their own way. Liberals commonly argue that government is too passive and does not promote enough progressive change—or that when it does act, it favors the interests of the powerful and wealthy. Conservatives believe that government is inherently inefficient and wasteful, and thus should do as little as possible. Conservatives accuse liberals of risking the (workable) present for some yet unproven vision of the future, which is supposed to be achieved with the help of government. According to conservatives, the more active and powerful the government becomes, the more undemocratic the government becomes. They believe "the government that governs best is the government that governs least." When conservatives advocate change, it is usually **regressive change**; that is, they want to regain something good that was previously lost.

> "If a man is right, he can't be too radical; if he is wrong, he can't be too conservative."
>
> —Josh Billings

Because the term **progressive change** sounds positive, some people may confuse it with meaning "good." Whether progressive (or regressive) changes are good is in the eye of the beholder. In this sense, however, progressive change means reforms that are generally untried, innovative, and further in the direction of a particular goal that has not been reached. For example, the gradual extension of voting rights over the last two hundred years is an example of progressive change. Regressive change refers to a return to a prior standard or policy, a renewal, or perhaps an attempt to counteract the erosion of a valued idea. Deregulation of private business is in most cases an example of regressive change. It attempts to reverse the gradual and progressive regulation of business over the years and return that part of the market to free enterprise principles.

Liberals point out that conservatives are most likely to be the "haves" of society, and they accuse conservatives of attempting to preserve their unfair dominance over the "have-nots." Liberal change is most commonly an attempt to help the "have-nots" gain more political or economic power, thereby promoting more equality. In other cases, liberals accuse conservatives of complacency in the face of problems—in other words, they say conservatives are unwilling to face the reality of the future. In either case, liberals think that an active government is essential in promoting equality and solving problems.

One of the most basic differences between liberals and conservatives concerns economics. Conservatives have traditionally advocated a policy of *laissez-faire* (pronounced *lay-say-fair*). Laissez-faire is French for "allow to act," "leave alone," or "let it be"; it implies a minimal and passive role for the government in the economy. Liberals generally believe in a more positive economic role for government and believe it has a duty to responsibly manage economic problems. Liberals tend to support *progressive taxation* such as the bracketed personal income tax, which taxes wealthy individuals' income at a higher rate than others' income. Liberals arue that those who have benefited the most from society and can best afford taxation should pay a larger share. After all, they argue, the upper class largely controls the election process, government investments and priorities, the business world, the justice system, and so on— the (welfare) scraps from the table that society gives to the poor pale in comparison—so it is only fair that the wealthy be taxed at higher rates.

Conservatives generally oppose redistribution of wealth and power and believe that society, in its natural state, rewards those who work hard and punishes those who do not. They believe that tax policy should not be used to turn this natural state on its head. Conservatives therefore tend to support *regressive* or *proportional taxes*. Regressive taxes, like sales taxes, and especially excise taxes, tax the wealthy's income at a lower rate than the income of the poor. For example, the wealthy and the poor pay about the same amount of gasoline and tobacco taxes per person; this amount is a much smaller percentage of the wealthy individual's income. A proportional ("flat") tax is necessarily a tax on personal income because it would tax all individuals, regardless of income, at the same rate. These taxes, conservatives argue, do not punish hard work and success.

Likewise, conservatives generally oppose liberals' attempts to use government to further regulate the economy. Liberals justify regulation, or partial control, of the economy by saying it is necessary to promote the common good and protect society (especially the poorest members of society) from selfish, wealthy individuals. Conservatives argue that when the government intervenes in the marketplace it interferes with the efficient workings of free enterprise, bogging down initiative with its regulations and lowering productivity. In the long run, they say, this hurts everyone—even the poor. Liberals often point to the Great Depression of the 1930s as evidence of what can happen without adequate government regulation of the economy.

Lest the reader assume irreconcilable differences between liberals and conservatives on economic philosophy, it should be noted that common ground does exist. Few (if any) conservatives today advocate doing away with most economic regulations and government intervention; for example, liberals have been particularly successful with their arguments for regulation in the name of protecting the environment from overexploitation. Similarly, conservatives have successfully insisted that any attempt to regulate American businesses be weighed against the cost in lost profits and jobs, so that today's liberals also tend to act as protectors of big business. Further, in modern American elections, candidates from both dominant political parties begin with the assumption that the government is responsible for maintaining a healthy economy, and the voters continually reinforce this belief. Candidates are expected to offer solutions to "grow the economy," "create jobs," and so on.

So, although both liberals and conservatives advocate government action to remedy economic problems, they usually disagree about methods. Conservatives have traditionally tended to advocate passive policies that promote a profitable climate for private investors; liberals have traditionally relied more on government initiatives, such as education, job training, loans and subsidies, and public works. Generally the debate has concerned liberal attempts to incrementally add new laws and regulations and conservative attempts to chip away at existing laws and regulations. However, in recent years many influential conservatives have advocated more active government policies to encourage economic growth. A growing marketplace provides expanded opportunity for the lower and middle classes to stimulate the economy through the creation of small businesses and entrepreneurship—something that pleases liberals. Likewise, many influential liberals have begun to advocate government initiatives that are more in harmony with natural market forces, as conservatives have traditionally preached. This growing consensus has resulted in agreement on policies such as "enterprise zones," tax reform, and welfare reform.

Conservatives favor traditional social policies. That is, they tend to oppose evolving (deteriorating?) standards of public morality and believe that the government has a duty to protect society from what they consider to be the disintegration of social norms of behavior. This means strict enforcement of criminal law to deter crime. It means respect for and loyalty to established authorities. This includes upholding religious and moral values and practices as well as traditional sexual roles and norms. Most conservatives are not opposed to sexual equality in principle but often point to feminism and homosexuality as leading causes of the weakening of the American family. Many conservatives feel that liberals are too complacent about the erosion of traditional American "family values," which may contribute to increased crime, corruption, drug use, divorce, educational failure, immorality, and the replacement of the American work ethic with the cycle of welfare abuse and dependency.

Liberals tend to be suspicious of government attempts to act as a public guardian of social norms, believing that in most cases the government instead acts to establish norms and deprive individuals of personal choices and freedom. They argue for a strict separation of church and state, asserting that it is not the business of government to regulate personal morality, sexuality, or religious beliefs. Liberals often agree with conservatives' identification of social problems, but they usually believe the conservative cure is worse than the disease. For example, most liberals say that in fighting crime, one should never sacrifice individual liberty in the name of protecting the social order. Liberals are more likely to argue that social problems are rooted in social injustice, educational inequality, workplace discrimination, drug abuse, and the like. For example, whereas conservatives say that a lack of family values contributes to poverty, liberals say that poverty makes the promotion of family values more difficult. Liberals also claim that conservatives are intolerant of those who are not like themselves (typically racial minorities, religious minorities, homosexuals, working women, immigrants, the urban poor, etc.). Conservatives believe they are making a principled stand. In the 1992 presidential campaign, Vice President Dan Quayle made family values a campaign issue with his "Murphy Brown speech." (Murphy Brown was a television character who was soon to become an unwed mother. Quayle criticized the program's apparent portrayal of her situation as normal and acceptable.) In championing family values, then president George Bush spoke in relatively positive rhetorical terms, with more praise for good values than attacks on or criticism of dangers to family values. Polls initially indicated a fairly positive response to this theme until the Republican convention, when Pat Buchanan, Pat Robertson, and other more conservative speakers spoke in stronger, more negative terms—in rhetorical language that many party leaders later said "turned off" moderates. Liberals attacked the speeches as mean-spirited and even hateful.

The challenge for conservative candidates is to appeal to the core Republican Party constituency without seeming extreme or intolerant—without offending people. Conservative candidates must clearly blame social problems on liberal "permissiveness" rather than on racial minorities, religious minorities, homosexuals, working women, immigrants, the urban poor, and so on. For example, most conservatives say that unwed mothers, racial minorities, and the poor are not the *causes* of problems but the *victims* of failed liberal policies, however well intentioned, and that homosexuality, divorce, illegal immigration, religious diversity, and so on are the results of liberal permissiveness. The challenge for liberal candidates is to define liberalism in positive rhetorical terms, avoiding an association with permissiveness. Thus liberal candidates must put forth a positive agenda for combating social problems by appealing to the average voter's sympathy for educational opportunity, employment and job training, freedom of personal choice, civic duty, unity, social justice, and tolerance of differences. If they do not, conservative opponents will define liberalism as being "soft on crime," immoral, and indifferent to social ills.

Foreign policy is an area in which it has been more difficult to discern ideological positions, because cooperation between liberals and conservatives is probably greater in this area than in any other. When it comes to dealing with the outside world, Americans tend to unite behind common positions. In foreign policy issues where there is not such unity, differences are often nonideological; that is, there are both liberals and conservatives in each opposing group. However, it is possible to note differences, even though they may be less distinct than those in other policy areas.

During the cold war, conservatives were most concerned about the spread of communism and saw Soviet subversion as the root cause of revolution and chaos in developing countries, as well as most other foreign policy problems. Emphasizing the Soviet military threat, they discounted the use of diplomacy and international law and tended to see the world in *bipolar* terms (two-sided, without a neutral position). Conservatives promoted higher levels of defense spending and preparedness, U.S. military aid to anti-communist governments, and (occasionally) U.S. military intervention in foreign countries. Liberals emphasized international cooperation to address world problems and promoted arms control agreements with the Soviet Union. According to liberals, the root causes of revolution and disorder in developing countries were poverty, nationalism, and the lack of democratic institutions there. Liberals argued against supporting undemocratic countries during the cold war and tended to support economic aid rather than military aid or intervention.

According to liberals, conservatives were so fearful of the spread of communism that they could not accept change in the developing world, and so concerned with maintaining stable trade patterns and international markets that they could not see the injustice in impoverished countries. According to conservatives, liberals were blind to the grave danger posed by communism and the Soviet Union, and naive to put their faith in diplomacy and international organizations. They cited the appeasement of Hitler by the British and French, and the lack of preparedness of the United States to the Japanese attack on Pearl Harbor. The lessons of World War II, they said, were to avoid appeasement and be prepared—which translated into a distrust of diplomacy and arms control, and higher levels of defense spending. Today the end of the cold war has blurred the traditional positions of conservatives and liberals on foreign policy, although the differences cited here remain in most respects.

The Republican Party generally represents conservative positions today. The Democratic Party generally supports more liberal positions. These tendencies are especially notable in the case of better-informed party activists, such as those who attend political conventions and donate time and money. Those who are only marginally partisan are a more diverse group who tend to pick candidates on the basis of their perceived image, charisma, advertising, and so on rather than on the ideological values and issues for which their party and its candidates stand. They usually identify themselves as moderates. Therefore it is a mistake to associate all Republicans with all conservative causes and all Democrats with all liberal causes. For example, a large part of the Republican Party consists of those who support abortion rights (the liberal position). And

Table 2-1

Ideology of Voters by Self-Identification, 1996

	DEMOCRATIC DELEGATES	ALL DEMOCRATS	ALL VOTERS	ALL REPUBLICANS	REPUBLICAN DELEGATES
conservative	3%	16%	25%	43%	52%
moderate	47%	48%	46%	36%	19%
liberal	31%	31%	18%	8%	1%

SOURCE: Washington Post/ABC News telephone survey of 1,514 randomly selected adults, conducted August 1–5, 1996.

some of the most notable "cold warriors" were liberal Democrats (Truman, Kennedy, Johnson). Moreover, since the Great Depression the Democratic Party has always been quite diverse, being relatively conservative in the South, for example. Some Republican Party activists describe themselves as liberal, although they are more rare than conservative Democrats. Many people are difficult to label because they hold conservative positions on some issues and liberal positions on others. This illustrates an important point: the terms *liberal* and *conservative* are best used to describe policy positions rather than individuals.

Furthermore, many issues, especially issues involving foreign policy, defy liberal/conservative classification. Foreign trade policy is a good example. Protectionists (those opposed to free international trade) span the ideological spectrum, ranging from some of the most liberal members of Congress (often from states with active union members who feel threatened by free trade), to Ross Perot's followers, to isolationists, to social conservatives like Pat Buchanan. NAFTA (North Atlantic Free Trade Agreement) and GATT (General Agreement on Tarifffs and Trade), the free trade treaties recently completed by the Clinton Administrations, were supported by Carter but also by Nixon, Reagan, and Bush (and even Rush Limbaugh). Various liberal and conservative interest groups lined up on both sides of the trade treaties as well. Thus it is important to note that the terms *liberal* and *conservative* are of limited utility. They may even be considered counterproductive, because as crude labels they close debate and free thinking about issues and are used instead for ad hominem rhetoric (name-calling attacks on the speaker rather than on the speaker's actual argument).

DIVISIONS WITHIN THE LIBERAL AND CONSERVATIVE POSITIONS

The preceding discussion of American liberals and American conservatives describes their policy differences in a general sense but makes few distinctions within the categories of liberal and conservative. The purpose of this section is to describe some of the divisions within the liberal and conservative positions. Any division will be arbitrary, because there are as many distinct positions as there are individuals within a category. At any rate, there are at least four distinct types of American liberals: reform liberals, New Deal liberals, the New Left, and neo-liberals. There are at least four distinct categories of American conservatives: organic conservatives, laissez-faire conservatives, the New Right, and neo-conservatives. Each of these types is described below.

Reform Liberalism

Reform liberalism is the oldest and most comprehensive of the four types of American liberalism. Its advocates say it represents an unbroken path of evolution from the Founding Fathers' liberal ideals of freedom and individualism to today's modern liberalism and its ideals. Just as the American Founding Fathers struggled to perfect the art of government, reform liberals are continuing the effort. Reform liberalism has been expressed by the early Jacksonian Democrats, who extended voting rights and elections and better represented common men. After the Civil War, the Radical Republicans ended slavery and tried to promote equal protection for African Americans. At the turn of the century, the Progressives (in several political parties, including the Democrats and Republicans) reformed city governments, fought political corruption and inefficiency in government, promoted conservation of natural resources, championed women's right to vote, attacked consumer fraud (especially in the food and drug industries), promoted the rights of workers, and began regulating business in what they believed to be the public interest. During the 1950s and 1960s, liberal Democrats led the civil rights movement to end racial segregation, eliminate barriers to voting rights, and promote equality of opportunity for women and racial minorities. They also promoted civil liberties, such as freedom of expression, religion, assembly, and the rights of the accused. Today reform liberals are active on a number of additional fronts, including election reform, health care, education funding, environmentalism, consumer protection, and combating discrimination against the disabled, homosexuals, and the elderly.

New Deal Liberalism

New Deal liberalism has much common ground with reform liberalism, particularly in the area of economics. Franklin Roosevelt used the slogan *New Deal* in his 1932 presidential election campaign, to popularize his plan to end the Great Depression through more comprehensive economic regulation of the economy. The New Deal came to mean emergency relief, welfare programs, social security, public works (e.g., restoration of public lands and infrastructural developments), agricultural regulation to prevent overproduction, rural electrification, higher taxes on the wealthy, protection of labor's right to organize and bargain, regulation of banking and stocks and bonds, and a general attempt to reduce the instability of the boom and bust business cycle. This massive increase in the size of government convinced conservatives that Roosevelt was a radical bent on doing away with capitalism. Some of them called him a "Red" (a communist). However, his views were moderate compared to those of many politicians at the time, who accused him of doing little of importance. Roosevelt argued that through moderate reform he was trying to save capitalism (from revolution)—not destroy it.

Whereas reform liberals are more often white-collar professionals (some conservatives like to call them "limousine liberals"), New Deal liberalism was aimed at average blue-collar workers and came to be understood largely as the promotion of the interests of the working class and farmers. After the death of Roosevelt, New Deal liberals continued to believe that the government must take an active regulatory role in the economy and ensure a decent standard of living for average citizens. President Johnson campaigned for the building of the "Great Society," requiring a myriad of social programs designed to fight poverty, illiteracy, disease, and lack of opportunity. Critics of New Deal liberalism blame it for creating a wasteful "welfare state" that has damaged the competitiveness and efficiency of the American economy. Yet it has led to a permanent belief on the part of most Americans that the government is at least partially responsible for managing the economy and guaranteeing their welfare from all economic threats.

The New Left

The **New Left** was largely a phenomenon of the 1960s, and it represented only a small portion of all liberals. It grew primarily out of opposition to the Vietnam War. The New Left coalition also included feminists, socialists, anti-racists, pacifists, and various radical advocates for the poor and powerless. It was probably most influential on college campuses, where students were politicized by the Vietnam War and the civil rights movement. Although the New Left agreed with most of the basic goals of reformers and New Dealers, its approach was more radical. Many of those in the New Left were more suspicious of liberals than of conservatives, because they considered most liberals to be lukewarm and too cautious in their reform. After all, they argued, conservatives who did not clearly understand the world's problems could be excused for their indifference, but liberals could not be. The most serious disagreement with the New Dealers was probably over foreign policy, because the New Left rejected the Democratic cold warriors' anti-communism and military interventionism. Since the end of the Vietnam War, the New Left coalition has been splintered and rendered relatively ineffective as a political force.

It is possible that a "neo–New Left" could consolidate under the banner of post-materialism. *Materialism* in this sense means a focus on economic matters and private self-interest in particular; and, to a degree, a disinterest in spiritual, philosophical, and ethical values. Therefore, *post-materialism* suggests a movement that attempts to reverse the materialist mindset of modern capitalist society. Post-materialists argue that the pursuit of money and possessions has left us spiritless and without real meaning; instead, society should concern itself with social justice and harmony, equality, environmental protection, peace, and humanitarianism. The post-materialist movement is already fairly strong in Europe and can expect to find allies in the United States among reform liberals, the New Left, and even some conservatives who are less concerned about economic matters.

Neo-liberalism

Neo-liberalism, meaning "new liberalism," fully emerged in the early 1970s. It is popular among intellectuals who claim to be less ideological and more pragmatic. Its title implies rejection of traditional liberal ideology, especially of New Deal liberalism. This is partially true, but it is more accurate to say that neo-liberals have retained the goals of liberalism but advocate new methods of reaching them. Neo-liberals are more willing to consider approaches that New Deal liberals consider conservative. For example, neo-liberals argue that no government can pay for social programs and combat social problems unless there is a healthy, growing economy. In this view, members of the middle class would be willing to be taxed to pay for social programs only if their paychecks were increasing at a faster rate than their tax bills. Thus as a practical matter the first step to fighting poverty, inequality, and social injustice is to foster a growing economy. In other words, instead of re-slicing a shrinking pie, the liberal imperative should first be to create a larger pie.

Neo-liberals reject the hostility between New Deal liberals and the business class as counterproductive. Additionally, they argue that the other liberals' traditional responsiveness to the needs of organized labor, farmers, small businesses, racial minorities, and other organized interests has resulted in a neglect of the national interest. Similarly, neo-liberals believe liberalism's focus on the rights of the individual should not be allowed to override society's interests. They maintain that public policy should be based on good economics, not on political maneuvering by special interests and individuals.

In prescribing good economics, neo-liberals start with the premise that we live in a global economy. Policy that ignores the increasing role of international trade, law, and culture is outdated, they believe, and isolationism in economic affairs is impossible. Global competitiveness requires a reduction in military spending and a recognition that economic strength is a prerequisite to continued military strength. Because neo-liberals reject protectionism (policies that restrict free international trade), in their view the fundamental task of national government is the coordination and planning of what they call an *industrial policy* to make the United States productive, competitive, and flexible in the changing world economy. (Industrial policy is discussed in Chapter 5.) This requires extensive government investment in infrastructure, education, research and development, and a government-business relationship. These are things that require an active government, not one that passively watches from the bench as the conservatives would prescribe.

Organic Conservatism

Organic conservatism is the most direct descendent of classical conservatism. The metaphor *organic* comes from the idea of society as a living thing—as a unified whole rather than a collection of individuals. In this view the social "body" can only be correctly understood as a complex, fragile being that must be carefully nurtured. It is not, as liberals might believe, merely a device for the individual's self-improvement and convenience. In fact, society is more than individuals. It consists of groups, families, nations, classes, institutions, moral codes, tradition, heritage, religion, customs, and accumulated wisdom. Individuals have no meaning beyond their social context and relationships within the community. Additionally, individuals benefit from their society and as such owe certain civic obligations and duties in return. Organic conservatives believe the government constructed by liberals is "big" where it should not be (e.g., in promoting individual rights and legal entitlements, and in trying to solve social problems through law alone) and weak where it should be strong (e.g., in teaching ethical standards, and in maintaining the national character and sense of responsibility). This results in a continuing breakdown of social institutions, standards, and organization. Society must resist the liberals' notion that an individual sets his or her own moral standards.

According to organic conservatives, liberal government undermines long-term stability and security in the name of promoting equality and democracy, the obsessions of liberals. The excessive growth of democracy has led to politics by the interest groups that can scream the loudest, and by selfish individuals who have no sense of civic duty and the greater social good. Equality under the law is a worthy goal, but government should not try to force social equality, because inequality is natural. Social evolution and innovation, when necessary for the health of the social organism, should be carefully considered, slowly planned, and gradually implemented. When change occurs, government's most important functions are to prevent the erosion of public order and security, and to safeguard the citizens' sense of community.

Laissez-Faire Conservatism

Laissez-faire conservatism, according to its adherents, represents the remnants of classical liberalism applied to modern-day society. In fact, many of those who understand the history of ideology still call this philosophy liberalism (in the classical sense). To repeat, *laissez-faire* implies a minimal role for the government in the economy: maintaining national defense, enforcing contracts and protecting property, enforcing criminal justice, and little else. How did this brand of American conservatism descend from classical liberalism? Classical liberalism, with its advocacy of private property and free enterprise capitalism, has become the status quo of the American economy. Laissez-faire conservatism seeks to conserve that status quo—liberal capitalism—and protect it from modern liberals' constant attempts to regulate it. Alternatively, where regulation already exists, the laissez-faire conservatives fight to reverse it. According to them, modern liberals have abandoned free enterprise capitalism.

Like the classical liberals, laissez-faire conservatives celebrate individual liberty, not the organic whole of classical conservatives. They argue that competition among individuals as they pursue their private interests is both natural and good for society. Profit, wealth, and the accumulation of property is a natural measure of an individual's merit, and nothing should be done by government to interfere with that marketplace process. Progressive taxes on the rich only serve to punish success and thereby undermine the very processes that accumulate capital for reinvestment and new job creation. According to laissez-faire conservatives, the interest of entrepreneurs and business *is* the public interest;

they owe no other obligations to society. (Liberals who oppose them sometimes call them "country-club conservatives.")

The New Right

The **New Right** is a term used since the 1970s to describe those who mix social conservatism with religion. Although some people who agree with their agenda may do so for nonreligious reasons, religion is overwhelmingly the motivating force behind the movement; adherents sometimes call themselves the *Christian Right*. Most, but not all, are Protestant evangelicals and are sometimes called *fundamentalists* by the press. They argue that the American constitutional system is best understood through biblically based interpretation (an even higher constitutional standard, essentially) rather than through constantly evolving modern standards. Many consider the Founding Fathers divinely inspired (by God). Even though religion has always played a part in both liberal and conservative ideologies and political movements, the New Right is so much better organized, funded, and unified that it merits special attention. Although there are several organized interest groups that represent the New Right, the most important and politically powerful one is the *Christian Coalition*.

Many members of the New Right are former southern Democrats, and their entry into the Republican Party threatens the dominance of the laissez-faire conservatives of the party. The momentous struggle between the New Right and the laissez-faire conservatives for the heart of the Republican Party has prompted the use of the term *Old Right*, to label those (mainly laissez-faire conservative) Republicans who feel threatened by the New Right. (Members of the New Right sometimes refer to them as the "Neanderthal Right," "paleoconservatives," and [stealing from Spielberg] the "Jurassic Right.")

Unlike the other parts of the conservative wing, the New Right is primarily a lower- and middle-class mass movement. It appeals to common people, especially rural white Christians who are troubled by what they believe to be the moral disintegration of the country, and who believe the political elite is out of touch with mainstream America. Although they generally agree with other conservatives that the government taxes, regulates, and spends too much, economics is not really their battlefield. They are primarily concerned about social issues. Among the threats facing the United States, the New Right lists: abortion, drug abuse, pornography, homosexuality, feminism, divorce, birth control, immigration and the proliferation of foreign languages and cultures in the United States, socialism, pacifism and disarmament, international law and government, leniency in criminal justice, gun control, and secular education (especially the teaching of evolution rather than creationism in schools, and the prohibition of school-organized prayer).

Neo-Conservatism

Neo-conservatism, like neo-liberalism, emerged fully during the 1970s as an intellectual movement rather than a mass ideology. It developed partially as a reaction to the Great Society and the New Left; in fact, many neo-conservatives (often called "neo-cons") are self-described 1960s radicals who grew dissatisfied with the movement. It was primarily a social science–based academic movement at first, which tried to balance the liberals' passion for correcting social problems with moderate "humanistic conservatism."

Unlike the laissez-faire conservatives, neo-conservatives recognize the flaws of modern capitalism but agree that the liberals' remedies are even worse. They generally show more concern about poverty and unemployment than do the laissez-faire conservatives; but they agree that market forces, rather than the government, should solve economic problems. The difference is that neo-conservatives are more willing to use government to provide market incentives and create more opportunity, as long as government does not become a force of crude income redistribution from rich to poor, and as long as it does not create a welfare class that is dependent on the government. Neo-conservatives are not as anti-government as are laissez-faire conservatives. In this sense they are more like organic conservatives. In their view, government can be used for good if it promotes public morality and does not create excessive expectations for radical change. Like organic conservatives, neo-conservatives are concerned about the decline in standards, tradition, institutions, and respect for authority.

Neo-conservatives are probably most noted for their opposition to what they consider "social engineering," that is, attempts by government to change public opinion and behavior (especially to promote equality). They claim that liberal concern for equality of opportunity has today been twisted into an unrealistic demand for equality of results. They accuse modern liberals of being opposed to freedom, individualism, and capitalism, since each of these promotes inequalities. Neo-conservatives oppose affirmative action, comparable worth (government efforts to increase pay for jobs typically held by women), multiculturalism in education, and what they label *political correctness* (liberal intolerance of anti-equality sentiments or comments that liberals consider offensive)— each of which they believe is an attack on liberty. Some, but not all, neo-conservatives agree with the New Right's critique of social ills, although most would say the New Right exaggerates the problems. However, many neo-conservatives are disturbed by the tactics the New Right uses, which they see as a sort of right-wing political correctness.

Neo-conservatives have strong anti-communist roots, having emerged largely through opposition to the New Left's anti–Vietnam War campaign. They also opposed the New Left's policy of anti-interventionism (or what neo-conservatives considered pacifism) in other countries. Consistently, they were aggressive advocates of military interventionism during the Reagan administration.

In conclusion, although there is diversity of opinion among the liberal and conservative causes in the United States, it is also quite clear what unites each side. In each liberal group there is a passion for progressive change and reform: reform liberals promote democracy, equality, consumer rights, environmentalism, and so on; New Deal liberals extend lower- and middle-class economic security; the New Left wants a variety of radical changes; neo-liberals want new economic approaches and an industrial policy. In each conservative group, there is a cautious approach toward reform and an advocacy of regressive changes: organic conservatives want to renew the community and social institutions; laissez-faire conservatives want to deregulate the economy; the New Right longs to return to prior moral standards; and neo-conservatives are largely a reaction to the New Left.

THE LEFT-TO-RIGHT SPECTRUM

Anthropological evidence suggests that many ancient people ate primarily with their right hand, greeted each other with their right hand, and symbolically communicated with their right hand. For these reasons, they probably protected it and kept it cleaner than their left hand. There are references throughout recorded history, including in the Bible, that suggest the right hand or the right side of a person was more honorable than the left. Commanders of ancient armies routinely stationed themselves to the right of the main body of their soldiers. Similarly, in the early European parliaments the aristocratic noblemen were given the honor of sitting on the right side of the king. The commoners were seated on the left. Because the nobility were conservative, wanting to preserve their privilege, conservatism began to be associated with *the right*. Those with the most to gain by change were the commoners on *the left*; they were more liberal (in today's American terms). In the United States today, the left still relates to liberalism and the right remains associated with conservatism. Consistent with these terms, **moderates** are said to occupy *the center* of the spectrum (they are often called *centrists*).

If the right is associated with the status quo and represents the elites of a society, and if the left is associated with change and represents the commoners of a society, then one would expect the left to represent a larger share of the population in any given society. This is generally true of most countries; but in largely middle-class societies such as the United States, there is a level of contentment that ensures a fairly consistent balance between liberals, moderates, and conservatives. Additionally, the right is usually more united than the left in most countries. This is understandable, given the fact that reformers, although numerous, often do not agree with one another about the solutions for the problems they agree exist. Some commentators believe the left is inherently more self-critical than the right. Conservatives say this is because liberal ideas are poorly constructed on flimsy foundations; liberals say it shows a willingness to subject themselves to critical analysis. In the United States this is evident in the self-criticisms to which the Democratic Party constantly subjects itself, including the criticisms of Bill Clinton by fellow Democrats in Congress.

The left-to-right spectrum is a way of describing to what degree an ideology promotes change in a system. By including more terms, it can denote more extreme positions on the issue of change. Those who are "to the left" of liberals are often called **leftists**, or **left-wingers**—referring to the wing, or seating area, in the House of Parliament to the left of the speaker. (The term is thought to have been first used in the French Parliament immediately before the French Revolution.) Leftists favor more drastic or radical change and are sometimes called *radicals*—a term that over a century ago came to refer to socialists, communists, and anarchists. However, many also call those on the far right radicals, so the term has lost its specificity today. Even further to the left are **revolutionaries**, who are not satisfied with reform—even radical reform—but insist instead on completely overturning the status quo and rebuilding new institutions of government.

The Left-to-Right Spectrum

The Left		The Center		The Right	
Revolutionary	Leftist	Liberal	Moderate	Conservative	Right-winger	Reactionary

Whereas those to the left of liberals are usually called leftists, those to the right of conservatives are sometimes called **rightists**, but usually **right-wingers**, although these terms are synonymous. Conservatives are resistant to change but are not completely unwilling to consider reform. Right-wingers consistently fight against reforms and progressive change in society. On the far right are **reactionaries**, a term derived from the word *react* and first commonly used during the French Revolution.

Reactionaries are not against change; in fact, they promote change. However, it is a different kind of change—a regressive change, or a backlash against change. They are *reacting* to what they perceive to be negative, or even traitorous, changes; they want to reverse the losses caused by the left, in a sense "turning the clock back." The word *reactionary* is generally used as a derogatory term; it implies a lack of sophistication and an inability to think positively and in an original way.

One should keep in mind that these terms are meaningless unless they are put into the context of time and place. For example, simply knowing that Mr. X is a conservative tells us very little. If Mr. X lived in the former Soviet Union today, it would mean he was resistant to the economic and political reform continuing there. If Mr. X is an American, is he a modern-day American or someone who lived in 1860? If he lived in 1860, his notion of conservatism would be very different from that of a conservative in 1996; for example, the 1996 conservative's views on regulation of the economy might seem quite liberal to the 1860 conservative. Furthermore, if Mr. X lived in 1860, was he a Northerner or a Southerner? If he lived in Philadelphia, his conservatism might be best expressed in his views about the economy; if he lived in Atlanta, his conservatism might be especially reflected in his social views—for example, his views on slavery and the rights of women.

Former Soviet leader Mikhail Gorbachev also provides an excellent example of how the terms are used. When Gorbachev came into power in the Soviet Union and began speaking of his plans for reform of Soviet politics (*glasnost* and *democratizatsia*) and economics (*perestroika*), he quickly came to be viewed as an almost revolutionary leader, or at least a leftist by Soviet standards. Those Soviets who felt threatened by his plans—such as bureaucrats, party officials, and some military leaders—came to be called the conservatives. As conservative opposition to Gorbachev grew, he began to temper his rhetoric and postpone key reforms in order to avoid antagonizing the conservatives. Most of the world press began calling him a liberal, more or less implying that he advocated reform of the Soviet system but not its abolition. This apparent retreat by Gorbachev, coupled with new freedoms of speech and the press under *glasnost*, led to leftist opposition to Gorbachev. People such as Boris Yeltsin and Andrei Sakharov began accusing Gorbachev of moving too slowly. Whereas at first this opposition was only sporadic and ineffective, it grew to the point that Gorbachev began to be considered more of a moderate—in the center, trying to balance the forces of the left and right. In an attempt to placate the right, he appointed to key positions many of the conservatives who later plotted the 1991 coup attempt. This caused many of his closest allies (such as Eduard Shevardnadze) and the architects of *perestroika* and *glasnost* (such as Alexsandr Yakovlev) to desert him. Finally, as reformers begin to outpace Gorbachev, pushing for more radical measures, they finally begin calling Gorbachev himself a conservative, especially after the attempted coup. It is probably more accurate to say that Gorbachev was a liberal, and that the more leftist reformers called him conservative for rhetorical purposes, just as some American right-wingers such as Pat Buchanan called George Bush a liberal for compromising with Congress.

In the broad terms of world ideological history, there is very little difference between modern-day American conservatives and liberals. They agree with each other on the most basic tenets of the American system. In particular, George Bush, Bob Dole, and Bill Clinton are really much closer ideologically than most Americans recognize. Just as some right-wingers call Bush and Dole "closet liberals," some left-wingers are suspicious of Clinton and call him a conservative. More accurately, Bush and Dole are primarily laissez-faire conservatives, and Clinton is a combination reform liberal and neo-liberal. On the left-to-right spectrum, Bush and Dole would be placed somewhere on the line between moderate and conservative, and Clinton would be somewhere between liberal and moderate. The portrayal of Clinton as an "ultraliberal" by some conservatives shows how ambiguous these terms are, and how they are used for rhetorical purposes. Most foreigners see little difference between them in terms of actual policy. American liberals and conservatives actually represent slight variations of a broader modern American ideology. Both evolved primarily from the same philosophical movement—classical liberalism. The influence of radical ideology on American politics is minimal.

To repeat, those on the right generally advocate regressive change. Those on the left generally advocate progressive change. However, in some cases it may appear that the left is promoting the status quo, or a return to a previous policy or standard, and the right is advocating reform and new, untried ideas. This phenomenon is especially possible in the United States because almost all leaders, regardless of labels others apply to them, are relatively close to the ideological center. Such confusion is rare in countries that are more ideologically divided, where the positions of left and right are more distinct. It is also the result of electoral systems that result in frequent changes in leaders, because the newly elected leaders often reverse the policies of their predecessors.

Consider some of the changes President Clinton has promoted, some of which essentially try to return the country to pre-Reagan policies. Does this mean Clinton is advocating regressive change and, therefore, conservatism? The solution to the apparent contradiction is the understanding that Reagan's policies themselves represented a conservative reversal of liberal progressivism; Clinton's policies actually represent a return to liberalism. Therefore, when considering whether a change is progressive or regressive, one should note the longer history of the debate.

Finally, note the following disclaimer about the left-to-right spectrum: it is only two-dimensional, and it only connotes progressive and regressive change. It may, therefore, place ideologies or individuals that are very different from each other at roughly the same position on the spectrum. For example, a radical advocate of animal rights and a socialist might both be called leftists, even though the animal rights supporter may not support socialism and the socialist may not agree that animals have fundamental rights. An opponent of gun control and a tax resister might each be called right-wingers, even though the gun control opponent may gladly pay his taxes and the tax resister may favor gun control.

RECENT PRESIDENTIAL ELECTION CAMPAIGNS AND IDEOLOGY

At the 1988 Democratic National Convention, Michael Dukakis, the presidential nominee, said: "This election is not about ideology—it's about competence." He meant that whether he was a liberal or whether George Bush or Ronald Reagan were conservatives was not the most important issue—rather, it was who was most capable. He also implied that the Reagan administration's ideological perspective blinded it to the modern world. Further, he argued that the large number of administration officials accused of wrongdoing and Reagan's poor grasp of the details meant that the Reagan-Bush administration was incompetent. Implicitly, Dukakis was contrasting this to his image as a practical problem-solver as governor of Massachusetts.

Rather than run from the Reagan record, Bush embraced it and cast himself in Reagan's ideological image. Believing the country was fundamentally conservative, he set out to prove that ideology does matter to Americans. He succeeded in shifting attention away from Dukakis's image of competence as governor and back to Dukakis's liberalism. At the Republican National Convention he went through a list of Dukakis's liberal positions, saying that he disagreed with each one and believed in the conservative approach in each case. Ultimately, Bush's victory was partly owing to his success at convincing enough voters that Dukakis was not motivated by practical methods but by ideology. Inherently Bush was stealing Dukakis's line, saying that Dukakis was a liberal ideologue and not a successful problem-solver. Democrats argue that Bush's claims about Dukakis's record were misleading and could have been deflected, had Dukakis been a better campaigner. On the other hand, Republicans (and some conservative Democrats) say that Dukakis lost because he was simply too liberal, period. Just as the country was in a relatively liberal mood in the 1960s and early 1970s, in 1988 it was still in the conservative mood that began in the late 1970s—and Bush was clearly more conservative.

What both sides appear to believe is that Dukakis made a mistake in not defending liberalism earlier in the campaign. By trying to avoid the liberal label while Bush proudly proclaimed his conservatism, Dukakis may well have reinforced the current notion among some Americans that liberal is a dirty word. Although it is generally true that candidates who appear the most moderate (neither too liberal nor too conservative) tend to do better than those who appear too ideological, it is also apparent from the 1988 election that a candidate cannot appear to hide his or her ideology either.

Most polls taken in 1992 continued to indicate that by self-identification, there are more American conservatives than American liberals. Clinton did get the votes of some who consider themselves conservative, but not many. So how can we explain the election of Bill Clinton and the defeat of George Bush? Several theories are plausible. First, it is important to note the following: most polls indicate that when given a choice, many respondents will describe themselves as neither liberal nor conservative but as moderate. Similarly, when pollsters ask about partisanship, a large number of respondents will claim to be independents rather than Republicans, Democrats, or members of other parties. Furthermore, many who claim to be liberal or conservative have little understanding of how those terms translate into politics and issues.

Another possible factor is the Perot candidacy. Ross Perot definitely changed the nature of the campaign, although we will never know what would have happened without his candidacy, or which candidate lost the most votes because of him. Part of the confusion lies in the difficulty of identifying Perot's ideology, and from which side he took the most votes. Democrats point out that election-day exit polls showed that Clinton would have won a two-person race anyway, but it is possible that Perot's campaign drove votes away from Bush and contributed to Clinton's margin over Bush in two-way polls.

Some observers claim it could also be that Bush (or any other candidate) was doomed to lose, because of the recession. It is true that when the economy is growing the incumbent party tends to keep the White House, and when growth is slow or negative the challenger tends to win. Many Republicans blame the election defeat on poor campaign organization and Bush's failure to communicate his economic platform. They say he was passive and unconvincing and could have better defended his economic record—after all, the entire global economy was in recession.

Another explanation is the cyclical nature of the national ideological mood and the accompanying political party system. In the 1930s–1940s, liberalism was popular largely because of Franklin Roosevelt. During the 1950s, conservatism reasserted itself. During the 1960s and early 1970s, liberalism was again relatively popular, which presented a nearly impossible task for the 1964 Republican candidate, Barry Goldwater, who was called "Mr. Conservative." His opponent, Lyndon Johnson, managed to portray Goldwater's conservatism as extremist, forcing Goldwater to defend it (much like Dukakis and Clinton had to defend the liberal tag). It could be that the conservative mood of the late 1970s and 1980s is now beginning to lose steam, at least enough to allow a relatively moderate Democrat to win. Also, the Republican Party in 1992 was probably at least as ideologically divided as were the Democrats. During the 1980s, the Republican Party grew large enough to begin to suffer from internal divisions (moderates vs. conservatives), as did the Democrats in the 1950s–1960s (conservatives vs. moderates vs. liberals).

> ". . . extremism in the defense of liberty is no vice . . . moderation in the pursuit of justice is no virtue."
> —Barry Goldwater (1964)

Or perhaps Clinton learned well from Dukakis's mistakes. Clinton never made a special attempt to deny or retreat from liberalism, and in fact he argued forcefully for various liberal social policies. However, he made sure to communicate what most people consider conservative positions on some issues, such as capital punishment, welfare reform, and tax incentives to businesses. Because of his moderate record in Arkansas, the Republican campaign had a more difficult time tagging him with New Deal liberalism; he was also more successful than Dukakis at portraying himself as a neo-liberal. And in the midst of what the public believed to be an economic crisis, the voters were interested in picking a problem-solver, not an ideologue. Clinton responded to this by debating with Bush on his Arkansas record, rather than his ideology. In the end, Clinton won by convincing enough moderate and independent voters that he was a problem-solver, and a more credible problem-solver than Perot.

During the first half of Clinton's first term, his opponents were much more successful at portraying him ideologically.   In 1993, Clinton increased taxes on the rich while lowering them on the working poor, tried to reform health care, reversed a variety of Reagan and Bush executive orders, supported the rights of gays in the military, and promoted other liberal measures that drove down his popularity.   However, the economy grew continually during his first term, creating many new businesses and jobs, while the inflation rate remained low. The budget deficit was cut by 60 percent in actual dollars, and even more dramatically in comparison to the growing economy. Even in foreign and defense policy, wherein critics predicted disaster, there were notable successes. Compared to the recession-plagued Bush presidency, most Americans judged Clinton to be a competent problem-solver. Ironically, the 1994

Republican congressional victory also helped Clinton, allowing him to label Speaker of the House Newt Gingrich's "revolution" *extremist,* an ideological term which focus groups and polling revealed to be very damaging. On the other hand, Clinton is not wildly popular and and is even distrusted by many Americans. He is often criticized by his own supporters for his inconsistency and lack of direction, and for his willingness to compromise rather than state what he believes and fight for it. This vulnerability suggested a winning strategy for Republicans in 1996—to make ideology matter again. Had their nominee been the New Right social conservative Pat Buchanan or the neo-conservative Gingrich, this task might have been easier. However, these two men were too unpopular to unite the Republicans or be elected president. Bob Dole was well respected, but relatively nonideological and passionless, and therefore ill-equipped to win a battle with Clinton over ideology and vision. Both Clinton and Dole were perceived primarily as problem-solvers; therefore, Dole could not have won by portraying himself as an experienced Washington veteran. Congressional Republicans urged Dole to promote a Reaganesque ideological vision of laissez-faire economics and tax cuts. The New Right tried to push Dole toward a more ideological campaign on social and moral issues. In the end, Clinton's image as a problem-solver triumphed.

Key Terms

classical liberalism	New Deal liberalism	leftist, left-winger
classical conservatism	New Left	moderate
liberal	neo-liberalism	rightist, right-winger
conservative	organic conservatism	reactionary
regressive change	laissez-faire conservatism	revolutionary
progressive change	New Right	
reform liberalism	neo-conservatism	

Study Questions

1. What are the positions of American conservatives and liberals on various political issues?
2. What are the differences and similarities between the various parts of the liberal and conservative positions in the United States?
3. What is the relationship of the political left and right to the concept of change? How would one identify individual members of the left and the right in any given political system?
4. What are the ideological persuasions of Democrats, Republicans, and independents? Are there ideological differences between party activists and average voters?
5. What are the limits to the use of the terms *liberal* and *conservative?*
6. What are some examples of how ideology is shaping American politics today?

CHAPTER 3

SOCIAL IDEOLOGIES

Social ideologies concern how people relate to one another. How does an individual fit into society? How can individuals be grouped together or classified? How are the relationships between people in a community defined? What are the duties of the individual, and what are the duties of society? Broadly defined, social ideology could include political and economic relationships between individuals. This chapter, however, is limited to nonpolitical and noneconomic ideology.

NATIONALISM AND INTERNATIONALISM

Nationalism may be thought of as a social ideology. The word **nation** is derived from the Latin *nat*, which refers to birth, especially into a specific tribe. **Nationalism** is a unifying social consciousness that inspires loyalty to the group—a group of people that is based on some common perception of culture, ethnicity, religion, language, territory, or even history and future aspirations. A shared history of suffering and injustice is an especially powerful force for nationalism. An even deeper force is often mentioned by political psychologists—the need for identity, and in some cases the need for psychological compensation for an individual's lack of personal accomplishment or pride. Nationalists believe that the individual is fulfilled through identification with a *nation-state*: a sovereign, self-determining political unit that represents and protects the interest of a single nation.

A **state** is a government, usually of a sovereign country. A country is a more general concept, but most specifically signifies a geographic territory. To be *sovereign* is to recognize no higher authority, and to be self-governing. The American colonies called themselves states when asserting their political independence from the British king. Thus, although we call California a "state" (of the union), the word also means "government."

Most Americans understand nationalism as patriotism to one's state (the country and the government that rules it, assuming the government is supported by the people). However, it should be clearly understood that a nation is not the same as a state or country, even though the words are used interchangeably by most Americans. A nation is a people, a country is a geographic entity, and a state is a political entity. The United Nations (UN) might more appropriately be titled *the United States of the Earth* because states, not nations, are represented there. (Even before the Palestinian Liberation Organization began self-rule of Jericho and the Gaza strip in 1994—that is, even before it had territory—its state-in-exile was represented in the UN. There are many stateless nations, such as the Kurds and the Basques, that are not represented at all in the UN.) The American "nation" is so broadly defined as to blur the difference. There is some disagreement among Americans regarding to what extent the American nation should accept new immigrants and adapt to and recognize a multicultural nation. However, most Americans—white supremacists, black separatists, and religious extremists excluded—are generally willing to accept anyone of any race, language, religion, culture, and so on into the American nation, as long as he or she accepts fundamental American constitutional values. This is very unusual, and partly a consequence of our heritage as a nation of immigrants. The countries that are most like the United States in this respect, such as Canada, Brazil, and Cuba, are also Western Hemisphere multicultural immigrant nations. Elsewhere in the world, the nation and the country are more clearly distinct.

"Here is not merely a nation, but a teeming nation of nations."
—Walt Whitman

Some countries, like Japan, have a population that is composed almost entirely (over 99%) of one nation. If and when Korea is united, it too will be composed precisely of the Korean nation. Such countries are truly nation-states. Other examples include Denmark, Iceland, and Poland. Some nations are *multi-state*: the Arab nation is spread over many countries. On the other hand, in about one-third of the earth's countries there is no one nationality that constitutes a majority of the population. In *multinational states* (countries that are not true nation-states), nationalism does not correspond directly to the state or country. A nationalist may not consider all the citizens or inhabitants of his/her land to be members of the same nation; in fact, some members of this nation might live across the border, perhaps oppressed by another nation in another country. Therefore, nationalism does not always mean loyalty to one's country specifically. Nationalism can lead to unity or separatism, depending on the national makeup of a country.

Nationalists perceive something particular or special about their nation, or "their people," that separates them from all other people—something that merits their loyalty or even love. It is probably the most powerful ideological motivation today. (Revealingly, some Americans seem to be more disturbed by reports of flag-burning than violent crime!) The perception of a unique nation acts to promote cooperation and unity among the people of a nation. Criminologists note that when a country is invaded by an enemy, criminal behavior falls dramatically. Ironically, although people suffer great hardships during war, nationalism binds them together in a cooperative effort in a way that no legal code could ever match. Some patriots even sacrifice their lives for their nation.

> "Patriotism is the last refuge of a scoundrel."
> —Samuel Johnson (1775)

Precisely because it is so powerful, nationalism is sometimes cynically used to manipulate the public or to divert its attention from serious threats or opportunities. For example, in a matter of days the late Somali warlord Mohammed Farrah Aidid was able to turn many citizens of Mogadishu from supporters of the 1993 UN relief effort to angry mobs protesting "imperialism and aggression." Significantly, he was more successful in this endeavor among members of his own ethnic group within Somalia than among Somalis in general. Throughout history, individuals have tried to excuse lies and criminal deeds by claiming to have acted out of love for their nation. American revolutionaries spread rumors and lies about British atrocities in an effort to cultivate American nationalism among an initially reluctant population. Some politicians today explain that their illegal actions were "necessary to protect American national security interests."

Nationalism has been especially beneficial in unifying the people of the former colonies of European imperialist powers. It was critical to their anti-colonial struggle and claim to independence. In this sense, it is also sometimes called **liberation ideology**. During the 1960s and 1970s, the term *third world nationalist* was commonly used in the American press to refer to leaders of liberation movements in decolonizing countries. Great debates raged concerning whether revolutionaries such as Ho Chi Minh (in Vietnam) were primarily nationalists or communists. Were the Viet Cong communist ideologues, certain of the logic of Marx and Lenin (each of whom were strictly opposed to nationalism), or did Lenin's condemnation of imperialism (the expansionist foreign policies of capitalist powers) simply appeal to their nationalist fervor to be free of French, Chinese, Japanese, and American domination?

A similar argument is being waged today over **Islamic fundamentalism**, which is a media term for the movement by various groups across the Muslim world to return to societies based on the traditions of Islam, as interpreted by certain religious leaders' understanding of the Koran. (According to Islamic fundamentalists, the Koran, Islam's sacred writings, also prescribes government and law; it thus can serve as a constitution as well as a bible.) Fundamentalism is very divisive in some Muslim countries, such as Egypt, Libya, and Lebanon. It is probably most popular in Iran. Are Muslims attracted to Islamic fundamentalism because of its ideological and religious appeal, or because it is native and constitutes a rejection of foreign influence and the corruption that is generally believed to be associated with it? In other words, is it a fundamentally different ideological challenge to the world, or is it chiefly a manifestation of nationalism? Beyond the Muslim world, there are a variety of other political movements that also fall loosely into the category of nationalist ideologies: for example, Pan-African nationalists, Christian Marxists in Central America, Asian Maoists, and "narco-revolutionaries" in South America and Southeast Asia. Each of these movements prompts similar debates. The question for American foreign policy makers remains: Are revolutionaries in developing countries motivated primarily by nationalism—or some other ideology?

Unfortunately for many of these newly independent countries, the colonial powers that carved up Africa and Southern Asia often drew colonial borders with little respect for natural national boundaries. (Most colonial powers exercised the classic Roman strategy of divide and conquer, pitting the various national groups against one another by stirring up their mutual fears.) Thus independence resulted in new countries with borders that split nations into more than one country and forced together various national groups that did not want to be in the same country. In many cases, small tribes were united in one country with large nations that would come to dominate and repress them. This has led to many separatist movements, waged via political, terroristic, and military campaigns.

It should be noted that the term *nationalism* is used in this book in a broad sense to include what some other authors identify as **tribalism**.

Tribalism can be thought of as a subset of nationalism. It implies an even further reduction of a nation into subnational sets. (The word *tribe* is derived from the Latin *tribus*, which referred to the three divisions of the Roman people.) The term *tribalism* generally carries negative connotations, since tribalism tends to cause war and reduce countries to small, economically unviable territories. The genocidal killing in Rwanda in 1994 illustrates all too well the effects of tribalism. At any rate, beyond the negative rhetorical use of the term, tribalism differs little in substance from nationalism.

> "Nationalism is an infantile disease. It is the measles of mankind."
> —Albert Einstein

Therefore, just as nationalism unites people, it pits nations against one another. Nationalism has torn asunder the former Yugoslavia with tragic consequences for all national groups there and threatens to spill its poison across the borders into adjacent states. It is so powerful that it has motivated Serbs, Croats, and Muslims to slaughter the neighbors with whom they lived in peace a few years earlier because of their differing religion, language, or ethnic identification. Those that escaped the killing were driven away from their homes to an area of Bosnia where their own nation predominated. Such so-called **ethnic cleansing** that occurred under media scrutiny in Yugoslavia (especially by Serbians against Bosnian Muslims) also occurs periodically in a large number of African (e.g., Rwanda and Burundi) and Asian (e.g., Sri Lanka) countries, although it typically gets less attention from the mainstream American press.

Even worse, nationalists may feel that their nation is not simply different from other nations, but superior to them. When this is commonly perceived it characteristically leads to hostile relations, if not war. The clearest example of such "supernationalism" is **fascism**. The World War II leaders of Germany and Italy—Hitler and Mussolini—were both fascists who used concentrated doses of nationalism to unite their people and pit them against most of their neighbors. Hitler's definition of his self-proclaimed "Aryan nation" included many non-Germans (other Aryans in Europe) and excluded others who were German citizens (especially Jews). It culminated in racism, genocide, and war. At the core of fascism is an extreme form of nationalism. However, fascism is more than a nationalist ideology and will be discussed more fully in Chapter 9.

> "You'll never have a quiet world till you knock the patriotism out of the human race."
> —George Bernard Shaw

Internationalists perceive commonality among a wider body of people; that is, the human species. Indeed, internationalists point out the dangers of extreme nationalism, such as fascism. Internationalists also believe that separate nationalist movements are counterproductive, especially when understood to mean that all nations deserve their own sovereign state. Most internationalists are not opposed to the principle of national self-determination but do not believe that self-determination requires sovereign independence. If it did, the pursuit of the nation-state by all the world's peoples would result in endless conflict. And because even within nations there are differences, where would self-determination end? On the other hand, mutual cooperation would benefit all participants, especially in terms of trade and the maintenance of peace and security. In many ways, nations today are interdependent and face mutual problems that cannot be adequately addressed separately. Is the nation-state obsolete? Is nationalism counterproductive and even dangerous today? Does patriotism and loyalty to one's government deprive a person of individuality and free will? Can it be replaced with loyalty to and respect for humankind in general?

American internationalists advocate an expanded role for the United States. They argue it is America's duty to aid suffering people anywhere in the world, whether they suffer because of foreign aggression, internal repression, economic impoverishment, or famine. To do nothing in the face of genocide or starvation is morally indefensible, they say. Further, we should especially assist those who share our values, such as respect for democracy and human rights—just as other nations assist those who share their values.

According to nationalists, the United States should not waste its resources in a futile attempt to solve the world's problems, especially when domestic needs are so visible. It should not sacrifice its blood to be "the world's policeman" or to "make the world safe for capitalism and democracy." Wars in foreign lands are often entangling and develop unexpected complications. Internationalists respond by pointing out that foreign aid is oriented primarily toward bolstering U.S. defense and foreign policy goals and boosting exports. As for military intervention, they argue that it is sometimes wiser to act early than to allow security threats to grow.

Clearly, nationalism is dominant today. Most countries are still rough approximations of nation-states, and most individuals remain supremely loyal to their nations. However, internationalism appears to be growing. There is more communication and cultural exchange between nations now than ever before. Interest groups such as Greenpeace and Amnesty International have reached across borders, internationalizing their memberships and activities. Immigration between all countries of the world has mixed the earth's nations in an unprecedented manner. It is proba-

Foreign Aid

A recent poll revealed that Americans estimate foreign aid to be about 15 percent of the U.S. budget. In fact, the 1996 aid budget of $12.4 billion amounts to about three-fourths of 1 percent of the U.S. budget, or about one-sixth of 1 percent of the total American economy. In fact, only $7.3 billion of this amount is actually developmental assistance; the rest consists of military aid and export subsidies. Further, the entire 1996 international affairs budget of $18.6 billion (of which foreign aid is the biggest part) has been cut by 51 percent (in inflation-adjusted dollars) since 1984, creating tremendous difficulties for American diplomats and policymakers.

SOURCES: James Carroll, "Uncle Sam's New Stinginess," *Boston Globe,* July 23, 1996; *The Economic and Budget Outlook: Fiscal Years 1997–2006* (Washington: Congressional Budget Office, May 1996); Washington Post National Weekly Edition, July 22–28, 1996, p.7.

bly fair to say that many governments are finding it harder to keep their nations' support in wars fought in foreign countries. Some countries have joined together for trade purposes in economic unions or common markets, such as the European Economic Community, which is one part of the **European Union** (EU; formerly the European Community, or EC).

Fifteen states are currently members of the EU, and several others are pressing their applications. The EU has its own government, albeit a weak one with less relative power than that of the states that compose it. The EU includes a Council of Ministers, a European Court of Justice and a European Parliament. Voting coalitions in the European Parliament tend to be along trans-European party lines rather than state against state. Although at present most important decisions regarding the EU still are made by the executives and governments of each member state, the European Parliament is slowly growing in power and becoming more independent of the national governments. The EU today is more or less a confederation (a loose grouping of sovereign states), as was the United States until 1789. Many observers expect the EU to evolve into a federal government (with full sovereignty) in the near future.

Other examples of regional integration include the Organization of American States, the Arab League, the Organization of African States, the Association of Southeast Asian Nations, a few commodity cartels such as the Organization of Petroleum Exporting Countries, and many regional common markets in Latin America and Africa that promote free trade among members and coordinate economic policies vis-à-vis other countries. The United Nations, the closest thing to world government, is again growing in power and influence, rejuvenated by the end of the cold war. The growth of the United Nations is especially evident in its increasing role as a "peacemaker" (e.g., in Kuwait, Somalia, and the former Yugoslavia) as opposed to its traditional and more limited role as a "peacekeeper."

Beyond formal government organizations is the emergence of many very powerful **multinational corporations**. These corporations cannot truly be called American, British, Dutch, German, or Japanese, because they are owned by citizens and governments of many countries; they use materials, labor, and management from many countries; and they sell their products around the world. They have to a large degree helped unite the world, at least economically. Most observers believe that political and social ties tend to follow economic ties.

Reflecting on the end of the cold war and the growing interdependence of the nations of the earth, George Bush repeatedly used the term **New World Order**. Although he never precisely defined it, he probably intended it to summarize increasing internationalism, the growing effectiveness of the United Nations, the vital importance of trade, the growth of multinational corporations and international interest groups, the expanded role of international law, and the end of U.S.–Soviet hostility.

Confronting the growing internationalism in economic matters is a rising tide of **economic nationalism** in many countries, including the United States. American economic nationalists especially oppose the North American Free Trade Agreement (NAFTA) between the United States, Canada, and Mexico, and the General Agreement on Tariffs and Trade (GATT), which created the World Trade Organization. In 1992 and 1996 the Republican presidential candidate Pat Buchanan said we must "put America first," meaning essentially that we must protect American industry from foreign competition, especially Japanese. This would require tariffs, import quotas, and other trade restrictions and could possibly initiate a trade war.

Beyond protectionists, there are other nationalists who fear the United States is slowly giving up its sovereignty to a growing world government (the United Nations). They believe the New World Order is a stepping stone to a dictatorial regime of the future, which will deny Americans their freedom. However, few—if any—proponents of internationalism advocate a unitary world government with the power to deny nations their basic self-rule in local matters. Rather, they advocate some kind of federal or functional world government (a United Nations with limited sovereignty, solely concerning international affairs—or even more specifically, only over certain international regulatory functions such as trade, immigration, communications, transportation, etc.). Internationalists insist that world government is the only way to protect the earth's seas and atmosphere, fairly share the burden of aid for developing countries, slow population growth, conserve natural resources, promote free trade that is beneficial to all nations, and require equitable and peaceful resolutions of conflict.

ELITISM AND EGALITARIANISM

In Old French the word *élite* referred to the "chosen" or "selected"—thus the highest, or best. The elites are the most powerful members of a society. Although it certainly has political and economic overtones, **elitism** is primarily a social ideology. Essentially, elitism is the belief that there exists a better or more capable group of people in society, with education, intelligence, wealth, or even "proper breeding." This group, whether based on class, race, sex, or something else, is naturally superior to the rest of society and deserves to maintain its position, power, and benefits. Its members are also best able to govern, manage businesses, lead social organizations, and so on and should be rewarded for their "service" to society. Elitism may be relatively benign—the elites may be good rulers, acting in the best interests of the masses. More typically, elitism is repressive and exploitative—the elites act only in their own self-interest and exploit those they rule.

Those who believe in the superiority of one race over others (or the inferiority of certain races) are called **racists**. Those who believe in the superiority of one of the two genders are called **sexists**. Merely two generations ago a great many Americans held such views; today they are unpopular. Further, it has become socially unacceptable among most Americans to express these or other beliefs that even indirectly appear to reject the notion of social equality or that seem insulting or insensitive to various groups of people (a constraint that critics have labeled **political correctness**). Thus most modern American elitists claim to base their definition of the elite on education, intelligence, and relatively objective indications of ability. Most elitists claim that social inequality is natural and not a problem in need of correction by society or its government.

Egalitarianism, sometimes called **equalitarianism**, is the ideology of social and legal equality. Egalitarians do not believe in a "better class" of people. They believe that all citizens are potentially fit to govern. Most believe the distribution of privilege, power, respect, wealth, and everything that humans want should be based on merit rather than on birth, luck, or arbitrary decisions of rulers. Radical egalitarians go beyond simply advocating equality of opportunity and demand absolute equality as an end result—these people believe that inequality, for whatever reason, is a social ill that must be corrected.

It is often said that the American Founding Fathers were elitists. They derisively referred to egalitarianism, especially radical egalitarianism, as "leveling." This was particularly true of the federalists (Hamilton's faction, which became the Federalist Party) and less so of the anti-federalists (Jefferson's faction, which evolved into the Democratic-Republican Party). It is certainly true that they were all wealthy elites of American society, but the constitutional system they created reflects elements of both elitist and egalitarian thought. For example, although the right to vote was severely curtailed, the very notion of public elections was an egalitarian idea at the time, because European and Asian monarchs allowed few elections of any kind and certainly did not extend political power to "peasants."

Dominant American ideology blends the egalitarian notions of fairness, opportunity, and merit with the elitist notion of governance by those who are most capable. The federalists viewed themselves as an American aristocracy, fighting to preserve order against irresponsible radicals who could easily persuade the uneducated masses to vote for them. Jefferson defended what he called the "natural aristocracy," based on "virtue and talent." Conversely, "wealth and birth" were the grounds of an "artificial aristocracy." In other words, Jefferson argued that when the elite are selected by their merit and not by privilege, they are legitimate and society benefits from them. Thus he believed that a form of government should be created that promotes the emergence of a meritorious elite.

Some say American elitism is no longer based on "virtue and talent," if it ever was. The modern American elite is no longer a well-educated and thoughtful group of people like the Founding Fathers, they argue, but rather sports and cultural heroes, whose elite status is marketed with great sophistication like breakfast cereal or running shoes. Most Americans today who rise to positions of wealth and status feel no obligation to return to society a portion of their rewards. Compare this mentality to Chinese Confucianism: egalitarianism is perhaps not as strong in China because Confucianism teaches unequal relationships (such as emperor/subject, father/son, and student/teacher) to be normal. However, in Confucianism the superiors owe an obligation of *virtue*. It is the elites' responsibility to be virtuous in return for their privilege. This balance is rejected by most Americans, who believe that everyone should have an equal opportunity to rise to the top, upon which they owe little, if anything, to the others they passed by.

Which of the two, elitism or egalitarianism, is most dominant in the United States today? This is an extremely controversial question. Many of the hottest present-day debates rage over the question of equality, especially in terms of racial equality and **feminism**. Feminism is the ideological belief that women should enjoy the same political, economic, and social rights as do men. Practically all Americans today say they believe in equality (although most men *and women* say they are not feminists, probably because of the rhetorical overtones of the term); but when the question becomes one of specific remedies or policies, views diverge widely and there is little public consensus. Certainly the United States is relatively egalitarian in comparison with many other countries. For example, it is probably true that American women enjoy more social, political, and legal equality than any women in history (with the exception of ancient matriarchal societies). The United States has gone as far as any other country in guaranteeing legal and political equality by prohibiting discrimination on the basis of sex, race, ethnicity, religion, age, and disability. Of course, there are notable exceptions: the lack of a constitutional guarantee of gender equality, mandatory retirement in some cases for the elderly, the inability of unpopular religions to win legal recognition for property tax purposes, and so on. Moreover, many Americans claim that they cannot enjoy equality because few laws exist to protect homosexuals, the homeless, the overweight, the ill, smokers, the young, or others from discrimination.

But genuine social equality is difficult to achieve through political measures alone. Economic inequality intervenes, in the United States as elsewhere. A poor landless American citizen can vote today, just as a wealthy landowner can, but who would conclude that they have equal input into the selection of our government leaders? And despite years of civil rights legislation, no one can deny that sexism, racism, and other forms of discrimination persist both in the marketplace and in the hearts of Americans. As is often pointed out, social equality cannot be legislated. For example, the passage of the 1990 Americans with Disabilities Act will not prevent informal and unprovable discrimination against those with disabilities, just as other civil rights laws have not brought an end to social discrimination. No matter what the law says, inequalities continue. What can be done about that? As mentioned above, it is when remedies are suggested that opinion swiftly diverges. Many people are opposed to the inclusion of new groups of people, most notably homosexuals, in civil rights legislation. Others are opposed to affirmative action in favor of women, racial minorities, or the disabled. There is even increasing use of the term *speciesism* and demands that animals be protected from discrimination or unethical treatment. Of course, the belief that egalitarianism "has gone too far" is not new to the United States. What is today accepted was once also considered radical, such as abolition of slavery or the right of women to vote. These measures were resented in their time, and there was a backlash of resentment against them too. For the last two hundred years at least, egalitarianism has continued to grow in the United States—although whether it or elitism is dominant remains debatable.

Because it is relatively unpopular in the United States to be outspokenly elitist, the defenders of elitism rarely argue directly for inequality. The debate between elitists and egalitarians is more often expressed in terms of **procedural egalitarianism** versus **substantive egalitarianism**, (previously referred to as *radical egalitarianism*). Presuming a consensus in favor of promoting equality, which is the best way of achieving it? A procedural egalitarian believes that processes should be open

Majority-Minority Districts

The Voting Rights Act (VRA) requires state and local governments to draw districts in a manner that does not diminish the effective voting strength of racial minorities. The law was passed because many districting plans, especially in the southern states, had traditionally been drawn (gerrymandered) in such a way as to prevent minorities from being elected in significant numbers to representative bodies. This could be accomplished by *diluting* them into many districts so that their numbers were insignificant everywhere, or by *packing* them into one very populous district where they could not influence the others around them.

As originally written, the VRA outlawed *intentional* racial/ethnic gerrymandering, which theoretically should result in more minority representation. However, if districts are drawn without regard to race or ethnicity in areas that are well integrated, minorities will by definition be outnumbered and will consistently lose elections. This analysis assumes that citizens vote along racial/ethnic lines—which they do, in most cases. There are some states and cities where race-conscious voting is minimal, but in most districts it is strong. Therefore, in 1982 the VRA was amended to require that redistricting maps not have the *effect* of diminishing minority representation. This has resulted in the drawing of strange-looking (reverse) racial gerrymanders, called *majority-minority districts*, that are designed to include enough of a certain minority group to ensure that one of them wins the election. Such districts weave in and out of ethnic neighborhoods, segregating minorities from other districts. Supreme Court justice Sandra Day O'Connor compared one such district to apartheid. This segregation also tokenizes minorities as representatives of ethnic ghettos.

But what would be the result of racially blind districts? Clearly, as long as people vote along racial or ethnic lines, very few minorities would be elected. And in traditional at-large elections, it is even more difficult for minorities to be elected. Are there any other alternative election systems?

---

and fair. Discrimination that interferes with an equal opportunity to achieve must be rooted out by government. A procedural egalitarian will admit, however, that this may not lead to a perfectly equal society. Government assurances of equal opportunity may not be enough to overcome unfairness, arbitrariness, and discrimination that persist among individuals. A substantive egalitarian believes that what matters most is not the process, but the end result. Indeed, to be content with formal equal opportunity while informal inequality continues to rule is to be

Affirmative Action

Colloquially, *affirmative action* means the aggressive pursuit of civil rights and equal opportunity. Actually, it goes beyond the concept of equal opportunity, since it attempts to compensate for past and ongoing discrimination in the workplace, in admissions to schools, in contracting, and so on. Individuals who are a part of a group (usually racial minorities, women, or the disabled) that has historically been victimized by discrimination are the beneficiaries of affirmative action. In practice, it usually refers to *goals* (to hire or admit, for example, members of some targeted group), expanded *efforts to search for and recruit* a diverse group of applicants, *"considerations"* (slight preferences in formulaic decisions), or *set-asides* (reserving a small number of positions, contracts, etc. for the targeted group).

Proponents of affirmative action consider it a temporarily necessary remedy to counteract discrimination, both past and present. It allows us to be true to our democratic ideals of pluralism and equality. It enlarges the pool of citizens contributing to our society's success. It increases the supply of doctors, teachers, accountants, and other professionals in the minority community. It provides children with role models. Businesses find it provides the diversity that is critical for sales and consumer relations. Local governments find that diversity in the police department is essential if it is to be effective.

Opponents claim it is unfair to others, especially nondisabled white males. This leads to resentment and bitter feelings rather than social harmony. In fact, they say, was not the goal of the civil rights movement the elimination of such considerations, which compromise objectivity, in the workplace and other public places? Further, affirmative action stigmatizes and stereotypes all members of the beneficiary group; others claim they got their jobs/positions/contracts/ only because of affirmative action—and could not have gotten them otherwise. Once such a program is established it will be difficult to conclude, they argue, and we should never retreat into more ("reverse") discrimination to combat discrimination.

Must fire be fought with fire, or should we treat all individuals equally, even though some start with less practical opportunity than others? How long should victims of discrimination be willing to wait for individual attitudes to change, before society resorts to awkward remedies?

---

self-delusional. Substantive egalitarians believe in using "temporary" processes that may be distasteful to egalitarians (including themselves) but that more consistently result in a more egalitarian society. This means those traditionally without power and influence must be given extra consideration or help in order to ensure their equal assimilation into society and to protect them from those who are hostile to such a result. Procedural egalitarians think that improper (nonegalitarian) means, no matter how noble the purpose, tend to corrupt the ends.

To more clearly appreciate this complicated concept, consider the dilemmas posed by majority-minority districts and affirmative action (in the boxes on pages 43 and 44). Martin Luther King Jr.'s dream was to live in a society where individuals are judged by the content of their character rather than by arbitrary measures such as race. Yet long after the battle against blatant and formal racial discrimination has been largely won, discrimination continues, often in more subtle forms. By any objective measure, King's dream is unfilled. Proponents of racial affirmative action and majority-minority districts argue that race must be taken into account if one is truly serious about correcting inequities. The current direction of the U.S. Supreme Court is to strike down such procedures where race is the predominant factor, although the Court has made it clear that race can be one of several considerations.*

Probably one of the best explanations for the continuing American extension of (critics would say "obsession with") equality was first noted by the French philosopher Alexis de Tocqueville in *Democracy in America* (1835). The United States has extended equality slowly, incrementally, and by a constitutional process. The extension was overseen by, checked by, and even driven by the elites ("from above," modern political scientists would say). Such a process proved more durable than the fiercely egalitarian French Revolution (generally from below), which degenerated into chaos and violence against all. Many political scientists today agree that the most fundamental egalitarian changes occur through gradual (sometimes tortuously long), nonviolent political processes— such as the 1950s–1960s civil rights movement in the United States, or the Indian independence movement under Gandhi—rather than through civil war and revolution.

INDIVIDUALISM AND COMMUNALISM

At the core of **individualism** is respect for the rights and dignity of the individual in society, as opposed to the interests of society in general. Individualists believe that by protecting the liberty of the individual, the whole society is protected in effect, because society is made up of indi-

---

* For example, see *Bush, Governor of Texas, et. al. v. Vera et. al.* Docket 94-805. (June 13, 1996), and *Shaw, et. al. v. Hunt, Governor of North Carolina, et. al.* Docket 94-923. (June 13, 1996). The first is about affirmative action and the second is about districting—there have been many similar U.S. Supreme court rulings.

viduals. Individualism, as a social ideology, is interwoven with *libertarianism*, as a political ideology (discussed in Chapter 4).

Communalists, or **collectivists** (sometimes called *communitarians*), emphasize the needs of society, sometimes at the expense of the individual. Communalists (not to be confused with communists) believe that the interests of a few should not be allowed to interfere with the greater interests of the many.

Individualists start with the premise that the individual freely forms social obligations and organizations. Therefore, society and government exist merely to serve individuals. When there is a conflict, the individual's interests should take precedent. Furthermore, the individual is completely responsible for his or her own success, and those who fail have only themselves to blame. Individualists believe this sense of responsibility creates the most productive and efficient society. When rights and duties are shared, both are incompletely fulfilled.

> "It takes an entire village to raise one child."
>
> —African proverb

Communalists believe that individuals are born with inherent social responsibilities. In their view, it is the duty of all individuals to live in harmony with others and contribute to the success of the whole. A communalistic society generally guarantees a minimum level of security to its members. Beyond that, it is considered somewhat selfish to lobby for personal benefits and rights, because it tends to interfere with the process of perfecting the group's benefits and rights. In fact, in some languages there is not even an equivalent of the English word *I*; instead, individuals refer to themselves in passive forms only (e.g., reflexively.) Communalists believe that through cooperative efforts, almost all individuals benefit far more than they would have had they worked separately toward their goals, frequently coming into conflict with each other.

The United States is without doubt one of the most individualistic countries in the world. Historians often cite the frontier experience as a contributing factor to American individualism. Surely the communal spirit of the Pilgrims and Puritans remains as an influence, but it is most concentrated in New England where they settled—and even there it has been substantially diluted. This is evidenced, for example, in the decline in attendance and relevance of town meetings and other collective practices common in the New England states. However, the rights of the individual were paramount to the Founding Fathers, especially the Jeffersonians (the Democratic-Republican Party). This is eminently reflected in the Bill of Rights to the U.S. Constitution, which prohibits government infringements on the rights of the individual and requires the government to

Society or the Individual? A Difficult Decision

You are a judge. Before you are four accused murderers. You know
with absolute certainty that three of the accused are guilty of murder.
The three murderers are likely to kill again if you release them. You also
know with absolute certainty that one of the accused is perfectly innocent of any crime. Unfortunately, you don't know which one of them is
the innocent one, and the law only allows you two choices: you can execute all four of them, or release all four of them. Which do you choose?
If you release them, you are probably more of an individualist: you might
argue that the state can never sanction killing an innocent individual. If
you execute them, you are probably a communalist: you believe one
individual sacrifice is necessary for the greater good.

rigorously follow "due process" before denying an individual's right to
life, liberty, or property. The Bill of Rights and other constitutional guarantees of individual liberty, and later judicial interpretations of them, has
resulted in a system of law that places the rights of the individual above
the rights of society. Critics, especially conservatives, say that federal
judges have dangerously stretched the original intent of the Founding
Fathers' words beyond reasonable boundaries that protect society from
criminals and deviant individuals. In comparison with each of its allies in
Canada, Western Europe, and Japan, the United States endures about
three to eight times as much crime per capita. Visitors to the United States
are often amazed at the apparent lack of social order, established norms,
and respect for authority in the American way of life. Many foreigners are
shocked at how easy it is to buy pistols, automatic weapons, explosives,
dangerous chemicals, or even radar detectors—with which Americans
can more easily break the law. What to Americans is considered privacy
and independence is often considered chaos and dangerous irresponsi-
bility to foreigners.

American individualism is also evident in the dominant economic
ideology, capitalism (discussed in Chapter 5). A larger percentage of
property is privately owned in the United States than in any other developed capitalist country in the world. Americans often successfully resist
attempts to legislate how an individual property owner may use his or
her land, even when at odds with the greater public good. In the United
States, companies generally act independently from each other in a dog-
eat-dog style of competitiveness. In communalistic Japan, most companies belong to a *keiretsu*, a closely linked "family" of manufacturers, suppliers, and distributors that own large amounts of each others' stock and

cooperate loyally. Americans have also resisted public transportation, preferring instead the luxury of private automobiles—at great cost to society (increased levels of air pollution, traffic congestion, and fuel inefficiency). Compare this to Japanese commuter trains: during peak times, workers literally pack the train tight with riders, enduring a loss of individual space and dignity that would be unthinkable in the United States.

In many countries, a person's status is more dominantly defined by the collective of which he or she is a part; that is, one's personal prestige, benefits, and success are dependent on the group's status. This is somewhat true in the United States as well. Nonetheless, because the United States is a pluralistic country of immigrants and is so culturally diverse, there is a somewhat less clear standard or consensus determining exactly how to define our leading institutions and groups. Therefore, individuals seek status in a variety of unique ways, generally more independently than individuals in more communalistic societies. The one clear standard of status in the United States, some argue, is money: dollars provide an objective way of calculating achievement and worth.

There is generally a respect for, or at least a tolerance of, uniqueness in the United States that is less common in much of the world. In many countries, it is not uncommon for strangers on the street to "correct" each other by publicly criticizing each other's dress, appearance, speech, or behavior. Most Americans wouldn't dream of doing this. Consider the Russian babushka (grandmother) correcting a stranger's behavior, the Japanese disdain for nonconformity, the constraints on Muslim women's attire, and the greater respect shown to adults' customs and preferences by young people in traditional societies in Africa and Asia. Religious, social, and cultural boundaries are especially more clearly defined in less developed countries.

Although individualism reigns dominant in the United States today, there is a growing chorus of voices arguing for a reevaluation of the current imbalance between individualism and communalism. The scarcity of collectivist values is reflected in prison overcrowding, juvenile delinquency, broken families, voter apathy, and eroding educational standards (with predictable consequences for productivity). Some political commentators argue that the country is ripe for a leader who can mobilize a renewed spirit of community values, citizenship, volunteerism, and sacrifice and an assault on the social problems plaguing America. Such a movement would demand a restructuring of budgetary priorities as well as values. Conservatives could be challenged to support a progressive tax code, better job training and opportunity for the poor, more spending for children and their schools, effective handgun regulation, and less devotion to personal wealth and economic growth at any cost to the environment. Liberals could be challenged to demand law and order, respect for authority and social institutions, responsibility and discipline from

The Gross Domestic Product: The Sum Is Less than the Total of the Parts

The most commonly accepted measure of the United States' prosperity and welfare is the Gross Domestic Product (GDP). Theoretically, the GDP is the total monetary value of all goods and services produced within the country in one year. It assumes that the sum of all *individual* efforts reflects the health of the *whole* economy and society. But does it?

The GDP does not measure unpaid work, such as parenting, volunteering, community building, and preserving nature. Thus when parents pursue their careers at the expense of their children, the GDP goes up—not only because of the parents' careers, but because of the increased costs of day dare, tutors, and child psychiatrists. When children are babysat by the shallow values and mindless consumerism of television, their subsequent purchases lift the GDP. When volunteer efforts are abandoned, professionals must be paid, raising the GDP. When neighbors do not know each other, the GDP rises due to increased reliance on security services, alarms, and police costs. When an ecosystem is wrecked by development or overexploitation, the GDP goes up. It rises due to any and all monetary transactions, including transportation accidents, liability lawsuits, weather catastrophes, divorces, real estate scams, illnesses (medical costs), theft (police costs, insurance costs, replacement purchases), pollution (clean-up costs), and the like.

The GDP does not differentiate between socially desirable production and individual profit at the expense of society. It does not properly account for the costs associated with economic growth or the damage done to the environment, families, and neighborhoods. Yet it is usually cited by both liberals and conservatives as the primary measure of *progress*. What does this suggest about American individualism?

welfare beneficiaries, and replacement of the social ethic of entitlements and rights with one of duties and obligations. Such a program might appeal to liberals who believe that self-interested capitalists cannot solve all of our problems, and to conservatives who believe that Americans have lost their sense of values.

Key Terms

nation	Islamic fundamentalism
nationalism	tribalism
nation-state	ethnic cleansing
state	fascism
liberation ideology	internationalism

European Union

multinational corporation

New World Order

economic nationalism

elitism

racism

sexism

political correctness

egalitarianism, equalitarianism

feminism

procedural egalitarianism

substantive egalitarianism

individualism

communalism, collectivism

Study Questions

1. What is the difference between a nation, a state, and a country?
2. What are both the beneficial and detrimental effects of nationalism?
3. What examples illustrate how internationalism is growing today?
4. How does American ideology blend the notions of egalitarianism and elitism?
5. What are the positions of procedural egalitarians and substantive egalitarians on the issues of majority-minority districts and affirmative action, as explained in the boxes? Why?
6. Is individualism or communalism dominant in the United States? What is the effect of this dominance?

CHAPTER 4

POLITICAL IDEOLOGIES

DEMOCRACY

There are many interpretations of the meaning of the word **democracy**, and most people and governments claim to be democratic. The word originates from the Greek *demos*, meaning "people," and *kratia* (-cracy), which means "rule" or "government." Therefore, in simple terms it means rule by the people (of themselves). A more specific interpretation of the original Greek meaning is that *demos* referred to common people, or even the lower classes, as opposed to the elite, or *aristoi*. Thus democracy was rule by the middle and lower classes, instead of rule by the upper classes as in aristocracy. At any rate, to the degree the mass public controls the actions and policies of its own government, it may be called democratic.

But what does it mean for the people to rule? Which people? All people—including children, the insane, noncitizens, criminals, and the apathetic masses? Rule what, or how much? Rule how—with what powers? How are decisions to be made? What if the people disagree with each other? When these and other questions are considered, it is apparent just how vague the term *democracy* really is. Individualists argue that without free will for the individual to seek happiness in whatever way he/she sees fit, democracy is impossible, because the individual would be ruled by society rather than him/herself. Communalists argue that the essence of democracy is rule by the many, over the selfish interests of the individualistic few. Capitalists believe that free enterprise and the right to own property are fundamental democratic concepts. Socialists believe that the great inequality between the rich and poor, fostered by capitalism, is inherently undemocratic. Therefore, because of the wide variety of interpretations of democracy, it has little meaning as a specific ideology or government system. Instead, it is more useful in rhetorical debate to mean more or less what is ideal, because few people today are willing to openly argue against democracy.

Actually, the almost universally positive connotation of the word *democracy* is a relatively new phenomenon. Aristotle, analyzing the Greek city-states, noted that most democracies eventually degenerated into tyrannies. Later observers typically criticized the wisdom of allowing common (poorly educated) people to govern themselves and manage the state. In fact, most of the American Founding Fathers derided democracy, calling it "mobocracy" (Hamilton), "suicidal" (Adams), and "spectacles of turbulence and contention" (Madison). Their worst suspicions about "mob rule" seemed to have been realized in the bloody and democratic French Revolution. Hamilton called the democratic public "a great beast." Even today some caution that democracy, in its adherence to majority rule, has a built-in tendency to ignore minority rights, legality, and even constitutionality. This negative connotation of democracy is sometimes referred to as **majoritarianism**, or tyranny of the majority. John Stuart Mill called it "social tyranny."

Abraham Lincoln's description of American democracy—"of the people, by the people, for the people"—is perhaps the most strict. By these words, he seemed to imply that ideally three conditions must be fulfilled. First, the government leaders should not be of a separate class of elites; they should be *of* the (common) people. Second, government must be created, limited, and controlled *by* the people, rather than be unchecked and unresponsive. Third, government must act in the interests of the masses—*for* the people. Many relatively undemocratic governments today cite solely the third condition as evidence of their democratic nature, as if to argue that as long as they produce results that are in the interests of their people, they should be excused of their undemocratic processes (the second condition). Some also go to great lengths to glorify the common origins of their leaders (the first condition).

PLURALISM AND AUTHORITARIANISM

As for the political question of who rules whom, the terms *pluralism* and *authoritarianism* hold more specific meaning. For example, they can better address the question of how "democratic" a country is. They are inversely related to one another—the more pluralism exists, the less authoritarianism exists, and vice versa. In general, the more pluralism exists in a country, the more likely people are to agree that it is democratic.

Pluralism as an ideology values a wide diversity of freely competing interests—interests that compete for political power. In other words, pluralism promotes the wisdom of a fair and legitimate struggle among different sources of power, each trying to contribute to policy decisions. Plural means more than one. More than one what? Pluralism refers to many sources of (political) power: more than one branch of government (separation of powers), more than one level of government (federalism or confederalism), more than one governing official, more than one political party, more than one candidate in elections, more than one media source, more than one interest group, and so on. All these things tend to promote democracy by decentralizing power. It is important to note that pluralists believe that government should nurture a **marketplace of ideas**—that is, ideas should be allowed to freely circulate in public debate; theoretically, the best ideas of each participant will rise to the top and be adopted. Citizens may participate in politics by joining representative groups or parties, or by forming their own.

Authoritarianism promotes a concentration of power in the hands of a few. Authoritarians do not want diversity of opinion. They do not want "competitors" in policy making, whether they be within the government or from opposition political parties or interest groups. They argue that a concentration of power in the hands of a strong executive (or ruling party, or military junta) is necessary to avoid the "inefficiency" of pluralism. With authoritarian rule there is decisiveness and consistency in policy making, which makes the country more stable, they say. There are no distractions such as public debate, demonstrations, or protests to divide the country and retard the work of the rulers. Thus authoritarianism is marked by concentration of government power, few (if any) multi-candidate elections, a government-controlled press (or at least strict censorship), prohibition of independent interest groups and parties, and usually a strong and unchecked executive (often a military leader).

Authoritarians often attempt to justify their rule by arguing that the stability and political predictability that authoritarian rule brings is necessary for developing countries. In their view, less-developed countries cannot waste time with partisan bickering and careening back and forth between the left and right, when the country simply needs to proceed forward with economic development. Others believe that it is actually pluralism that creates the best environment for growth and development—after all, are not most of the most developed countries also those with the highest levels of pluralism? Recently, three economists published the results of their research of the literature concerning this question.* They surveyed sixteen studies, each of which investigated the link between the rate of economic growth and the political system of various countries. Three studies found a positive correlation between pluralism and growth, three found a positive correlation between authoritarianism and growth, and ten were inconclusive. The authors conclude that growth is rooted in stability, but that the stability of a country depends on many factors other than pluralism and authoritarianism. It may also be a question of the long-term stability of pluralistic societies versus the short-term stability of authoritarianism. Pluralistic countries sometimes go through fluctuations of political turmoil, gridlock, or reversals in policy due to elections. Authoritarian countries are more likely to avoid such minor problems, but when change does boil over it is more likely to be drastic and violent.

PLURALIST IDEOLOGIES

Even though pluralism appears to be most desirable to Americans, some warn against **hyperpluralism**, or excessive dispersion of power among so many competing interests that there is never any consensus on what is to be done. In recent years the number of actors competing for political power in each policy area has continually grown, so that the institutions of government are less and less effective at authoritatively making policy. Many Americans say that special interest groups have become too powerful and unconcerned with the good of the whole society. This creates divisiveness and inconsistencies in policy as every interest selfishly tries to grab power. The result is not a neatly divided "political pie" that everyone has contributed to and shares in, but a compromised mess of ingredients that is hacked to pieces as everyone fights over disproportionately large shares. American hyperpluralism is the result of more than two hundred years of growth and evolution of interest groups, or what the founders called *factions*. The selfish tendencies of factions, and how to control them, was a major concern in 1787 and remains so today.

Hyperpluralism may also be a problem in relatively young political systems, for a different reason. In immature political systems, there is sometimes a free-for-all competition for popularity that results in no real

---

* Borner, Brunetti, and Weder, *Political Credibility and Economic Development*, Macmillan Press, 1995.

authoritative consensus as to the ideological direction of the country. In 1995 hyperpluralism reached its peak in Russia: 42 political parties fielded candidates for the parliamentary election, out of a total of 262 parties registered with the Russian Justice Ministry.

> "The government is best which governs not at all."
> —Henry David Thoreau

Hyperpluralism extended to its logical extreme would result in no concentration of political authority in any form, causing anarchy. **Anarchism** is thus the extreme end-point of pluralism. The literal meaning of the root word is "leaderless" (*an* means "without," *arch* means "leader"). Anarchists, believing that government is inherently corrupt and incapable of being reformed, advocate revolution to replace present institutions with self-rule. How would the new society be free of corruption? Good question—anarchists are often faulted for their lack of specificity and vague prescriptions. Some anarchists (anarcho-syndicalists), impressed by the turn-of-the-century trade unions, believed that unions (syndicates) could replace government. However, most anarchists believe that all forms of government and social organizations, including unions, that have leadership and law are exploitative and inherently evil. Human nature, on the other hand, they see as inherently good; but institutions, traditions, and rigid laws they see as tending to destroy human creativity and limiting possibilities. If only the stagnant, coercive institutions of society were removed or at least severely limited, people could live together in peace and harmony.

Many modern anarchists have taken inspiration from the Internet and the proliferation of home computers. The Internet is a global network of computer modem links. Because it is not centrally organized or managed by any government or company, it is a virtually uncontrolled worldwide information system, used for communication, research, advertising, and entertainment. As such, it is an ideal method for anarchists in the promotion of their cause.

Anarchism, as an ideology, advocates the beliefs outlined above. However, it is difficult to imagine anarchism as a real political system, since it would by its very nature be constantly in revolution—no institutions of government (of authority) could ever emerge. Dispersion of power would be so complete that government could not exist; because everyone would be directly competing for political power, there would be absolutely no concentration of power. Thus anarchism may be thought of as a theoretical end-point on a scale of pluralism, which could never actually be reached. However, many rhetorically use the term *anarchism* to identify a relatively great breakdown of political authority and order, such as that which existed in Lebanon during the 1980s or Rwanda in 1994.

Anarchism is often confused with **nihilism**. Nihilists claim to believe in nothing, whence the term comes. Nihilism is sometimes associated with anarchism because both reject social institutions and government. However, anarchists have a vision of social harmony whereas nihilists reject any kind of values, codes, or ethical judgments and supposedly favor the state of nature. Additionally, anarchists are not necessarily violent or terroristic; nihilists are. Ted Kaczynski, if he is the Unabomber as suspected, could probably be described as a nihilist, although in his manifesto (see p. 57), published in 1996, he calls himself an anarchist. The Unabomber's manifesto is full of contempt for modern industrial society and its associated ills. Most of the manifesto is about the effect that technology has on nature, social organization, free will, and the human psyche itself. It criticizes leftists for creating a powerful government that tries to solve all social problems but creates more in the process of repressing individuality. It calls conservatives "fools" for failing to understand that the rapid technological progress and economic growth they support is the very cause of the decay of traditional values that "they whine about."

Some argue that **direct democracy** would be relatively anarchic. Direct, or *pure*, democracy implies that citizens make policy decisions themselves, by voting, rather than by delegating that responsibility to their representatives. Of course, it is hard to imagine direct democracy on a large scale, with the mass public making policy daily. However, some forms of direct democracy exist already—namely, town meetings, the referendum, the initiative, the recall, and perhaps jury duty. Ross Perot has said he would govern in part through the use of the "electronic town meeting." Some suggest that in this computer age, all home telephones (or the fiber-optic cable systems of the future) could be equipped with some form of voting machine by which citizens could vote on all major issues. (Whether this would be advisable is another issue!)

One alternative to direct democracy is republicanism. One should not confuse republicanism with the ideas of the Republican Party specifically, just as one should not assume that the Democratic Party is the only American party that believes in democracy, or that the Libertarian Party is the only party that believes in liberty. These parties have simply named themselves after the ideological terms.

Republicanism is the ideology of indirect, or representative, democracy. Citizens participate by voting for their representatives, signing petitions, writing letters to representatives, contributing money to candidates and parties, joining interest groups, and so on. Republicanism takes many forms. It may promote leaders who are highly representative of the public, or it may favor an elite class of people who are hardly in touch with their constituents but simply give the appearance of being "of

Excerpts from the "Unabomber Manifesto"

The Industrial Revolution and its consequences have been a disaster for the human race. . . . they have destabilized society, have made life unfulfilling, have subjected human beings to indignities, have led to widespread psychological suffering . . . and have inflicted severe damage on the natural world. . . . We therefore advocate a revolution against the industrial system. . . . Among the abnormal conditions present in modern industrial society are excessive density of population, isolation of man from nature, excessive rapidity of social change and the break-down of natural small-scale communities such as the extended family, the village or the tribe. . . . The modern individual . . . is threatened by many things against which he is helpless; nuclear accidents, carcinogens in food, environmental pollution, war, increasing taxes, invasion of his privacy by large organizations, nation-wide social or economic phenomena that may disrupt his way of life. . . . Freedom means having . . . the power to control the circumstances of one's own life. . . . technology will eventually acquire something approaching complete control over human behavior. . . . The technophiles are hopelessly naive (or self-deceiving) in their understanding of social problems. . . . when large changes, even seemingly beneficial ones, are introduced into a society, they lead to a long sequence of other changes, most of which are impossible to predict. . . . in their attempt to end poverty and disease, engineer docile, happy personalities and so forth, the technophiles will create social systems that are terribly troubled. . . . The positive ideal that we propose is . . . WILD nature . . .

---

the people." Representatives may act as *delegates* whose job it is to merely reflect the wishes of their constituents, or as *trustees* who are expected to use their knowledge and insight to act in the best interests of the people, regardless of what the people actually think.

The framers of the U.S. Constitution favored republicanism, not direct democracy; that is, they created a system whereby the mass public would elect representatives, presumably "educated men of principle and property" (elites). In fact, as the Constitution was originally adopted, only members of the House of Representatives were directly elected (senators were elected by state legislators, presidents were chosen by electors, judges were appointed). Furthermore, few Americans actually had the right to vote: in most states, only property-owning white males over age 21 who were long-time residents of the state could do so. In the early nineteenth century, as the notion of democracy grew more popular, these voting barriers began to fall. President Andrew Jackson, elected in 1828, championed the commoner. His party, formerly named the Democratic-Republican Party, was renamed the Democratic Party. (Historians refer to this period as the era of Jacksonian Democracy.) Today the presidential and senatorial elections are more direct, voting rights have been extended to most Americans, and political and social equality has advanced considerably. Therefore, one may say that the United States has become more democratic and less republican since 1789.

> "The greatest freedom of speech [is] the greatest safety, because if a man is a fool, the best thing to do is to encourage him to advertise the fact by speaking."
>
> —Woodrow Wilson

Libertarianism, as a political ideology, focuses on individual liberty as a key to democracy. Libertarians are concerned less with how they are represented and more with limitations on their leaders' powers. Specifically, they want to maximize their self-rule by minimizing the government's power to interfere with their lives or make laws that dictate their political and moral values. The Founding Fathers' libertarianism is best expressed in the U.S. Bill of Rights (guarantees of freedom of speech, press, religion, assembly, petition, due process, criminal defense, etc.). Most modern libertarians, such as the members of the American Civil Liberties Union (ACLU), are primarily concerned with protecting these constitutional rights.

A smaller but somewhat significant group is the Libertarian Party, which advocates a much smaller government and the abolition of many laws that they consider to be unnecessary intrusions on the people's liberty—such as laws governing what they consider "victimless crimes" or personal ethical choices (abortion, drugs, prostitution, pornography, etc.). Like the ACLU, the Libertarian Party insists on a strict interpretation of political and social liberties. Unlike the ACLU, the Libertarian Party also advocates extreme economic freedom; that is, a government that does not collect an income tax, does not regulate the economy, provides no government subsidies to industry and no welfare assistance to individuals. The Libertarian Party may be considered socially liberal but economically conservative. At any rate, it consistently sees very little room for government authority. For this reason, its members are close to the position of anarchists.

Populism, from the same Latin root as the word *people*, may be thought of as the ideology of the commoner, or "the little guy." It refers to mass political movements organized at the grassroots level, often in rural areas or among the urban poor. It often arises owing to the perception that government is not truly representative of the common people—that the powerful government of the urban elites is not responsive to the needs of the poor or rural people. Populists tend to distrust the business and political elites of society, whom they consider to be authoritarians monopolizing political power. Pluralism to populists means letting the little guy also have a say in politics, and opening up policy making to more people than just the urban elites. Populists resent the implication that politics is too complex for rural people, the working class, and the poor to understand. Populist movements are often led by charismatic leaders who are able to stir the emotions of many people, including those who were previously not politically active, and transform them into a strong political force.

Historically, rural populism in the United States has tended to be a conservative populism, typically a reaction to government bureaucracy, taxes, and interference in agriculture or other local affairs such as education or religious matters. Urban populism has generally been liberal; the urban poor have felt that the status quo is stacked against them—they have been excluded from politics, and government does not act in their interests. Occasionally, charismatic populist leaders have found a way to unite the two. For example, in the 1988 Democratic presidential primaries Jesse Jackson tried to build such a coalition, of rural people (especially farmers) and the urban poor, along with others who said they "wanted to send a message." Other populist movements include the farmers' Populist Party of the late 1800s, the followers of Louisiana's Huey Long during the Depression, George Wallace's American Party of 1968, and the Citizens Party of the 1970s. The best-known American populists today are Ross Perot and Jesse Jackson.

Critics of populist movements accuse the typically charismatic leader of manipulating mass sentiment through exaggerations and demagoguery (passionate appeals to emotions and prejudices), feeding on their fears and lack of understanding of the complexity of government, and offering overly simplistic solutions. These critics sometimes point to fascism as an example of what can happen when charismatic, populist leaders come to power. This criticism was most recently leveled at David Duke (a former Ku Klux Klan leader) during his unsuccessful bid for the Louisiana governorship. Whether it is accurate to label Duke a fascist is a matter of opinion. At any rate, this does not mean that all populists are demagogues or fascists.

AUTHORITARIAN IDEOLOGIES

To repeat, authoritarianism concentrates political power in the hands of a few—rather than the many, as in the case of pluralism. Authoritarianism stands in opposition to democracy and pluralism. However, in some cases it is difficult to label a political system or idea as clearly pluralistic or clearly authoritarian. Some argue that even American republicanism is too elitist and therefore not very democratic at all, although this is a highly controversial charge. Perhaps it depends on just how representative these elites are. For example, some American leftists argue that pluralism in American politics rarely means more than pluralism among the *Power Elite*—the government, military, and business elite. On the other hand, right-wingers sometimes counter that the federal government is run by an elite of government bureaucrats and liberal academics. Either way, the implication is that there is little pluralism in American politics. These claims are not very popular; most observers say the United States is highly pluralistic. So what *does* more clearly constitute authoritarianism?

Monarchism (*mono* means "one," *arch* means "leader") is the ideology that legitimizes the absolute power of a hereditary ruler (usually a king or queen). The ruler is often said to be ordained or chosen by God, which is the chief justification for survival of the system. When the rulers are said to be gods themselves, or representatives of God or the gods, the ideology is called **theocratism** (*theo* means "god," *crat* means "ruler"). A theocrat believes that civil law should be based as much as possible on religious codes, values, and revelations. The theocratic monarch and his/her family is often said to be of particularly noble or aristocratic blood, an elite status that no one else in the society shares. The case of Iran today is unusual in that it is a theocracy without a monarchy. In Iran, the hereditary elite was overthrown by supporters of the religious leader Ayatollah Ruholla Khomeini. Although Khomeini never formally became part of the new Iranian government, all decisions were subject to his approval as Iran reconstituted itself as an Islamic theocracy, subject to Khomeini's interpretation of the *shari'ah* (law of the Koran).

Constitutional monarchism also concentrates authoritarian power in a monarch's hands. However, it is not unlimited power—some minimal restraints are imposed on the monarch by a constitution, and there exists a pseudo-representative body of aristocrats with very limited legislative powers, usually subject to the monarch's veto. Still other governments, such as the British, are constitutional monarchies in name only. The British monarch is only a figurehead; the real authority lies with an elected Parliament, which means the monarchy is not really an authoritarian form of government.

The most common forms of authoritarianism today are right-wing *military dictatorships* and left-wing *one-party states*. Rebel military officers typically seize power by force (in a military coup), by attacking the capital city and the forces guarding the central government's leaders. Sometimes merely the threat of violence is enough to bring down the

government, when it when perceives a lack of support for its continued
rule. The rebel officers then proceed to govern the country through martial (military) law. The American Founding Fathers clearly recognized the
danger of a politicized military and preferred citizen militias to a standing army, although they gave Congress the power to "raise and support"
one, should the need arise. Some social scientists argue that World
War II and the ensuing cold war steadily increased the political influence
of the American military, as a permanent *national security state* emerged.
Even President Eisenhower warned of the increasing political power of
the "military-industrial complex." It is certainly true that the U.S. military
is more politically active today, especially in terms of budget battles.
However, it has a long tradition of political neutrality and most observers
believe it is still unthinkable that the American military could threaten the
government.

One-party states are ruled by a single political party. If other political parties are allowed to exist at all, they are usually constrained by
unfair electoral rules that make it impossible to challenge the ruling party.
As such, minor parties are reduced to the equivalent role of weak interest
groups. The ruling party is also not equivalent to the American political
party; that is, its function goes far beyond recruitment of candidates and
election campaigns, to the actual administration of government.

One-party states are often the result of a military coup when rebel
leaders have an organized political party, as in the case of Saddam
Hussein of Iraq. Each may be ruled by an autocrat (a single "strong-
man"), in which case the political system is sometimes also called **autocratism**. Alternatively, each may be ruled by a group of leaders (a military *junta* or the top-ranking members of the party). Sometimes a military dictatorship, one-party state, or another form of autocratism has popular support and is judged by the majority to be serving the country's best
interests. Singapore is an example of such a **benevolent dictatorship**.
When the authoritarianism is not considered benevolent (as is much
more common), it is sometimes referred to as **despotism**. Military dictatorships are often rhetorically called fascist, whereas one-party states
are often rhetorically called totalitarian; both labels are extreme and are
in most cases inaccurate.

Totalitarianism is the theoretical end-point of authoritarianism. As
a political system, it would mean the complete (total) concentration of all
authority and total control over all aspects of society and government by
a single dictator. The totalitarian state would effectively replace all previous forms of social organization, such as independent schools, parties,
churches, unions, social clubs, and the like, as the single agent of socialization and education. Such unrestricted, unlimited government power
is also called **absolutism**. According to totalitarians, this absolute power
is legitimate because it is used to great effect on behalf of the people.

Would You Like to Live in Singapore?

Singapore has full employment, clean streets, very little crime, honest parliamentary elections, and almost no people living in poverty. Ninety percent of the population own their own homes. Most people are relatively satisfied with their government and its leader, Lee Kuan Yew. Singapore also has one-party rule and represses any who attempt to run against the ruling party or attempt to speak out or publish against it. The government restricts labor organizing, press freedom, and assemblies of more than five people. Its police detain individuals indefinitely without trial and interrogate prisoners with brutal methods. Heavy fines are levied for chewing gum or failing to flush a public toilet. Other crimes are punishable by a beating with a rattan cane. Possession of marijuana is punishable by death. Amnesty International and other human rights organizations are not allowed to operate there.

With no checks and balances to hinder government, they argue that the totalitarian state would be unmatched in power and efficient purposefulness.

As anarchism is devoid of authoritarianism, totalitarianism is devoid of any element of political pluralism, or democracy. Like anarchism, totalitarianism is a well-understood ideological concept, but there has never been a state that was totally ruled by one person—there are elements of pluralism even in countries that are often called totalitarian. In practice, therefore, the term *totalitarianism* is used to emphasize extreme authoritarianism, autocratism, and absolutism.

What is the fundamental difference between totalitarianism and extreme authoritarianism? Authoritarianism requires only a passive and obedient public. Totalitarianism requires active participation in and agreement with the state's ideology and policies. Authoritarianism can co-exist with a number of other cultural, economic, religious, and social ideas. Totalitarianism demands the complete attention of society. Thus any ideas that interfere with this goal are considered cancerous and must be ruthlessly eradicated. Totalitarians manipulate art, music, religion, history, architecture, and even symbolism to maintain absolute control. All aspects of society are controlled by one comprehensive ideology.

The meaning of totalitarianism is to a large degree historically defined, specifically by Nazi Germany under Hitler and the former Soviet Union under Stalin. Although Hitler's and Stalin's social and economic ideologies were very different, their maintenance of political power through terror and a secret police was quite similar. Furthermore, each

◄— PLURALISM   AUTHORITARIANISM —►
O—————————————————————————————————————O
Anarchism   **Totalitarianism**

was motivated by highly ideological theories, albeit different ones. In Germany, the Nazi Party ruled (supposedly in the name of the Aryan people) and Hitler ruled the Nazi Party, through the Gestapo (secret police). In the Soviet Union, the Communist Party ruled (supposedly in the name of the working class) and Stalin ruled the Communist Party, through the NKVD (secret police). In both cases all power stemmed from one autocrat. At the time, each was simultaneously feared and loved by most of their citizens. In both cases the fanatical allegiance to their leadership, writings, speeches, and ideological symbols strikingly resembled the faith and devotion of members of a religious cult.

With Hitler and Stalin in mind, in 1948 George Orwell wrote his famous novel *1984* about a future totalitarian society in which "Big Brother" (the dictator) ruled everything absolutely. All activities of individuals were constantly monitored, including their private lives—through the use of cameras in their homes. Even emotions and thoughts were controlled through the use of drugs. Was Orwell's vision accurate? Increasing technology *has* allowed governments to collect and record more and more information about their citizens. It has created incredible capabilities for electronic surveillance, propaganda, and computer files that record the lifestyles, characteristics, finances, spending, and opinions of the citizenry. (Some commentators say that we have even more to fear from "Little Brothers," meaning the hundreds of private insurance, credit, consumer research, marketing, and other companies that collect and sell information about people's private lives.) However, the information age, with its shortwave radios, satellite dishes, telexes, fax machines, and computer modems, has made it impossible for governments to completely control information, and therefore the consciousness and opinions of its citizens. For example, the Chinese government was for the most part frustrated in its attempt to hide the truth about its crackdown on the democracy movement in Tiananmen Square in 1989, and the leaders of the 1991 Soviet coup attempt did not even make a significant effort to control the news.

During the cold war, the term *totalitarianism* was often mistakenly used synonymously with communism, socialism, Marxism, Leninism, or the Soviet system in general. The leader of the Russian Revolution, Lenin (who died in 1924), and the Soviet leaders that followed Stalin (who died in 1953), may be called authoritarians of varying degrees, but not totalitarians—as Stalin can correctly be called. For example, some say Lenin advocated a "totalitarian party," which is not true. In fact, the term did not even emerge into popular usage until 1932, when the Italian fascist

Mussolini declared himself a totalitarian and Italy a totalitarian state. Italian fascism was authoritarian at a minimum, but historians may debate whether it was truly totalitarian. On the other hand, Nazism and Stalinism were clearly worthy of being labeled totalitarian. After the death of Stalin a limited form of pluralism (within the party and government) began to grow in the Soviet Union, although American political scientists were slow to recognize it and wrote little about it until the 1970s.

These terms had a special meaning for some cold warriors; for them, authoritarians were anti-communist military strongmen, and totalitarians were communists. Former Reagan administration official Jeane Kirkpatrick has said that authoritarians are preferable to totalitarians—by this she meant she would rather see a military dictatorship than a communist revolution. These are not the standard definitions used by most political scientists and historians, but the terms are occasionally used in this way—especially by those who consider themselves "anti-communists," including some liberals.

Today, authoritarianism is on the retreat around the world, not only in the former Soviet Union and Eastern Europe but in South Africa, Latin America, South Asia, and elsewhere. *Democracy movements* have emerged into full view in Middle Eastern monarchies and dictatorships. Multiparty systems are evolving in most newly independent African countries. Parliaments are replacing military leaders in many Asian countries. Most observers think the remaining authoritarian governments cannot survive much longer without reform or revolution.

Key Terms

democracy	libertarianism
majoritarianism	populism
pluralism	monarchism
marketplace of ideas	theocratism
authoritarianism	constitutional monarchism
hyperpluralism	autocratism
anarchism	benevolent dictatorship
nihilism	despotism
direct/pure democracy	totalitarianism
republicanism	absolutism

Study Questions

1. What are the root words of the ideological terms listed above, and how do they help explain their meaning?
2. Why is the definition of the term *democracy* so hard to agree upon in practice?
3. Is the United States a true democracy?

4. What was the Founding Fathers' view of democracy and republicanism?
5. What determines whether a political system is basically pluralist or authoritarian?
6. What is the difference between Democrats, Republicans, and Libertarians on the one hand, and democrats, republicans, and libertarians on the other?
7. What famous Americans are called populists, and why?
8. What kinds of authoritarianism exist?
9. Are totalitarianism and anarchism practical systems, or do they mainly describe systems only in theory? Why? How are the terms used in practice?
10. Were George Orwell's predictions accurate and warranted by changing technology?
11. Is communism the same thing as totalitarianism?
12. What is the difference between authoritarianism and totalitarianism?

CHAPTER 5

ECONOMIC
IDEOLOGIES

ECONOMICS AND POLITICS

Ideological thought concerning political freedom and democracy should not be confused with economic ideology. One of the most common mistakes by Americans is the assumption that the opposite of democracy is socialism (or communism). Similarly, students in socialist countries often mistakenly say that capitalism is undemocratic. Capitalists and socialists may argue that there is a connection between their economic beliefs and democracy, but in the eyes of most political scientists this is a very contentious argument. Economic ideology is not about freedom and the governing of the political world—it is about the control of production, distribution, and consumption of goods and services.

CAPITALISM AND SOCIALISM

The distinguishing characteristic of **capitalism** as an economic system is *private* ownership of property. As an ideology, it is the belief that private ownership and the free market constitute the most productive and fair economic system.   Capitalists believe that the marketplace is self-regulating and in need of no government interference. The laws of **supply and demand** regulate the market, encouraging investors (capitalists) to meet (supply) the needs (demands) of consumers. Moreover, **self-interest** will provide an incentive to work hard. Modern genetic research suggests that selfish behavior is the unsurprising result of thousands of years of natural selection; genes that do not promote selfishness do not tend to survive and replicate themselves in the gene pool.* Therefore, capitalism harnesses a natural human tendency: capitalists, with the incentive of maximizing their profit-making, will invest their capital in goods and services that are most in demand. This amounts to a self-regulating mechanism for planning future production. Furthermore, competition among suppliers ensures constant improvement in the demanded products and guarantees that prices will be as low as possible. (If the quality is poor or the price is too high, the consumer can turn to a competitor.)

The distinguishing characteristic of **socialism** as an economic system is *public* (or government, or state) ownership of property. Theoretically, the people collectively own all the means of production (nonpersonal property, such as factories, land, banks, and businesses) and control it through their government. As such, government is the only employer and guarantees a job and a minimum standard of living for everyone. As an ideology, socialism is the belief that society (rather than individual investors) should own property collectively, control the marketplace, and plan economic investments that will shape a stable, progressive future economy. Socialists believe that the capitalists' profit-making through their ownership of the means of production is exploitative and unfair to the working class.

Socialists believe that an unregulated economy is chaotic, or anarchic—the lack of stability caused by the natural fluctuations of the capitalist market causes unemployment and a waste of resources. However, they generally do not deny the productivity of the capitalist incentive motive, although they typically equate it with selfish greed. Even if greed is "natural," can it not be overcome? Moreover, they say, the reliance on the self-interest of the private investor alone may be efficient in supplying consumer demand in the short term, but it neglects the long-term best interests of society. For example, capitalism is much more likely to quickly create a supply for a consumer product, such as a new style of eyeglasses, that is suddenly fashionable (in high demand)—investors will quickly produce and market it, in order to cash in on the profit. However, making new styles of eyeglasses every season (thereby causing old styles to become obsolete and unsalable) hardly does much to

---

* *Source*: Richard Dawkins, *The Selfish Gene*, new edition (Oxford: Oxford University Press, 1989).

advance society. Capitalism is excellent in supplying pet rocks, automobile radar detectors, switchblades, and electric sock-warmers, but it can be argued that these products do not guarantee a better society. Similarly, the millions of dollars that the makers of Coke and Pepsi spend on marketing and advertising, all for the purpose of persuading consumers to choose from between what are practically identical products, is an incredible waste of resources from a socialist point of view. Furthermore, private investors are often unwilling to undertake socially useful functions that are not very profitable in the relatively short term (mass transit, recycling, low-cost housing, preventive health care, etc. are commonly cited examples).

In the United States today, health care is arguably the most obvious *market failure*; that is, the typical supply and demand constraints of capitalism do not operate well in the health industry. Consumers are poorly informed about the product (e.g., drugs, tests, surgery) and rarely question costs or procedures. The myriad of insurance programs complicates the market without providing much benefit normally associated with competition (the insurance industry reportedly accounts for roughly 20–25% of the total cost of American health care). Those without insurance are denied inexpensive preventative care until later, when they are provided with expensive emergency room treatment at public expense. Liability lawsuits and expensive new technologies have driven prices ever higher and have bankrupted families whose insurance coverage was exhausted.

"Capitalists privatize profits and socialize losses."

—Unknown

In other cases, private investors exploit and damage common resources (e.g., the environment) in order to make a quick profit for themselves. Often the capitalist maximizes profit by passing on costs to society in general, such as through taxes to build the infrastructure required for the capitalist's business, or by seeking government tax breaks, aid, and bail-outs when business is bad.

Rather than relying on the profit motive to guide the economy, socialists advocate a **planned economy** in which the government makes investments to meet social needs on a "rational" basis, according to socialists. Most important, central planning focuses on long-term development rather than market demands, which are inherently short-term. The government planning agency also sets prices, not necessarily based on the cost of production but on social need. Typically, essentials such as food and shelter are highly subsidized and are priced at much lower levels than their real cost of production warrants. On the other hand, luxuries such as automobiles and entertainment are priced much higher than their cost of production to make up the difference. In this way, resources are not squandered by the demands of the rich for nonessential production while basic human needs go unmet. In most socialist countries education and health care are free, or at least highly subsidized. Through controlling the numbers of students admitted into each field of higher education, the planning institutions try to plan the labor market as well, to coincide with the capital investments they make in new industry.

Criticism of socialism centers around three issues: lessened incentive, lack of responsiveness to consumer demands, and the cumbersome planning bureaucracy. The incentive to work hard is not totally missing in socialism—most socialist countries have a limited degree of incentive pay and bonuses, but it is not nearly comparable to what exists in capitalist countries. Further, since managers do not own the businesses they work for, they feel less responsible for their success—except to meet their *quotas*. (The yearly plan tells each state enterprise how much it is expected to produce for that year.) Generally speaking, the more a state enterprise produces in a socialist country, the more it is expected to produce in the future. Therefore, managers and employees have little desire to exceed the plan; if they did, it would be raised the following year. In the former Soviet Union it was common to see certain enterprises, such as bookstores, "closed for repairs" at the end of the month; having exceeded their quota by a respectable few percentage points (enough to win a small bonus), they closed to avoid exceeding it by too much. Often, meeting the quotas means simply turning out products; it has little to do with the quality of those products.

"We pretend to work, and they pretend to pay us."

—Soviet joke

The example of Soviet bookstores may remind the reader of what sometimes happens in American manufacturing when the workers feel they are being unfairly "speeded up" and respond with a "slowdown." There is a tremendous difference, however—such tactics, if practiced for very long, would threaten the American company with a loss of profit or even bankruptcy. In a socialist economy these practices may continue indeterminately.

In capitalist countries, it is said that "supply chases demand"; that is, investors attempt to satisfy the market demand to make a profit. Critics of socialism say that in socialist countries "demand chases supply"; that is, there is never enough of the products (especially consumer products) that the people want. This is primarily because government planners, operating without concern for profit, are slower to recognize demand;

moreover, they do not have to respond to a demand if they feel it is not "truly needed." This is less wasteful than chasing demand, because in some socialist countries the products are quickly bought when produced, keeping inventories low. However, consumers would obviously prefer to have more responsiveness to their demands for quality products and enough of them. It should be noted, however, that scarcity of consumer goods is not much of a problem in socialist countries that are relatively pluralistic (such as Sweden), but it is a problem in those that are authoritarian (such as China), so this lack of responsiveness to the public is probably more a result of authoritarianism than of socialism. The economies of authoritarian countries that practice socialist planning are often called **command economies**, implying that production is carried out at the command of the planning authorities rather than through incentive. On the other hand, there is also a great deal of planning in France (of both state-owned and private businesses), but private enterprises generally enter into voluntary agreements with the planning authorities.

Finally, critics of socialism point to the large planning bureaucracy that attempts to run the economy. Planning an entire economy is an incredibly complex affair. One of the traditional problems of central planning is how to set targets or quotas in such a way as to accurately measure the performance of an enterprise. Typically the plan would call for a certain quantity of the product to be produced, but this does not take into account quality, style, and consumer preference. As long as the firm meets its quota, it is judged to be performing properly. Because it has little incentive to give consumers what they want, the result is that consumers may refuse to buy the product. In a capitalist market, such careless plans would force the producer into bankruptcy; supply and demand ensures that businesses produce what the public wants.

Because all elements of a planned economy are interwoven, a failure in one sector of the economy can jeopardize all others. For example, if there is a miscalculation or production failure in the rubber industry, not enough tires are produced, which causes shortages in truck production, which means transportation bottlenecks, which means that less raw materials such as iron ore can be transported to processing, which means failure in the steel industry, which means less construction, and so on. Proponents of capitalism note that in a capitalist country the moment that the demand in the rubber industry becomes apparent, investors would jump in to increase production. This is more difficult in a rigidly planned economy.

Furthermore, pricing products without regard to their true cost of production leads to a variety of economic problems. For example, private farmers in the former Soviet Union commonly bought bread to feed to their livestock, because bread was artificially priced below cost, whereas lower-quality feed grain was not. This taxed the Soviet economy unnecessarily and contributed to occasional bread shortages as well.

The Petersburg Pajama Plan

During one particularly cold winter, local authorities in Leningrad (now St. Petersburg, Russia) were besieged with complaints that there were not enough pajamas (an item that is important in cold climates!) for sale. Authorities devised a plan to generously reward the clothing manufacturer that exceeded its monthly quotas on pajamas by the greatest percentage, a plan that would pit local pajama producers against each other in a contest to quickly produce as many as possible. To ensure quality, material standards were specified so the pajamas would be warm, comfortable, and durable. Did it work? A tremendous quantity of good pajamas was produced within the month. However, almost all of them were babies' pajamas (which required less material and therefore had a lower cost of production).

Despite the problems identified above, the Soviet and Chinese economies grew at tremendous rates under central planning until the 1970s. Most American economists concede that command-style planning offers at least some advantages for the process of rapid industrialization of less-developed economies. Whether it is appropriate for a modern post-industrial economy is a much less popular contention.

THE MIXED ECONOMY

It should be obvious from the preceding discussion that neither capitalism nor socialism are without flaws. For this reason most governments try to use what they consider to be the best elements of each. This is called a **mixed economy**; it is sometimes referred to as *mixed capitalism* in the case of basically capitalist economies, and *mixed socialism* in the case of basically socialist economies. No country in the world is purely capitalist or purely socialist. In the United States, for example, the Postal Service and Amtrak are government-owned and many cities own their electric companies and transportation services. Still other *natural monopolies*, such as telephone companies, are privately owned but highly regulated. These examples of public ownership and regulation, plus welfare programs and Social Security, are sometimes derogatorily called "creeping socialism" by their opponents. However, the United States owns a much smaller share of its industry than do Western European and other basically capitalist countries. The United States also taxes its citizens and businesses less and spends less per capita than other capitalist countries.

Russian Views of Capitalism

Market reforms should be . . .

continued:	30%
halted:	27%
don't know:	42%

Which economic system is better?

state planning/control:	36%
private property/market:	27%
don't know:	37%

SOURCE: Richard Rose, cited in *American Enterprise*, July/August 1996, p. 57. (Two thousand residents across Russia were polled in January 1996.)

In the former Soviet Union, even before the Gorbachev era, a significant quantity (about one-fourth of the total) of agricultural products was produced on private plots, which, along with surplus from collective farms, was legally sold on the free market (for much higher prices). Under Gorbachev's economic reforms, many more small businesses were created and legally registered under private owners (although they were highly regulated). The Soviets even opened a rudimentary stock market. Some of the same things have happened in China as well. Does this represent "creeping capitalism"? At the time of this writing, privatization is continuing in Russia and the other former Soviet republics, although it is unclear to what degree socialism will be replaced by capitalism. It is highly likely that a large element of socialism will remain, since opinion polls taken there now reveal less support for American-style capitalism than for the Western European model of a mixed economy.

VARIETIES OF CAPITALISM

Laissez-faire capitalism means unregulated, unrestricted, free enterprise. Laissez-faire ideologues believe the government's interference in the market is inherently bad and should be kept at an absolute minimum—no more than that which is necessary to protect the freedom of the marketplace. As noted earlier, *laissez-faire* literally means "allow to act," that is, "leave it [the market] alone." Its proponents believe that every rule and economic regulation that the government enacts detracts from the smooth operation of the market. Most of them cite the eighteenth-century Scottish economist Adam Smith as their intellectual father, although he was not as absolutist as are they.

Modern capitalism (sometimes called *regulated capitalism, Keynesian capitalism*, or even *post-Keynesian capitalism*) evolved as some of the abuses and inadequacies of laissez-faire capitalism became evident. For example, many blamed laissez-faire for allowing the emergence of large companies that destroyed all competitors and monopolized their trade. With the advent of antitrust laws (in the 1890s) that limited businesses' ability to monopolize and restrain trade, the economy began to be regulated. Other examples of regulation include child labor laws, health and safety laws, minimum wage laws, and pollution controls. The greatest change occurred in the 1930s under Franklin Roosevelt, as a response to the Great Depression. Roosevelt's New Deal was similar in many respects to the economic policies advocated by the British Liberal economist John Maynard Keynes, who suggested ways of stimulating the economy with government deficit spending to create jobs and end the economic depression. (It should be noted that present-day laissez-faire economists say the Great Depression was caused not by the lack of government controls but because controls had already begun to be applied—although this is certainly a minority view.) At any rate, today the government has a variety of tools at its disposal by which it can attempt to regulate the economy, by influencing the money supply, inflation, unemployment, interest rates, growth, foreign trade, and the like.

Not all modern capitalist economists are supporters of Keynesian theory. During the last twenty years several competing interpretations of capitalist philosophy arose to challenge Keynesianism, such as *monetarism* and *supply-side economics*. However, as evidenced by the criticism of President Bush about his alleged failure to act to end the recession in 1991–1992, few today in the United States question the basic responsibility of the government to manage the economy. Laissez-faire economists believe that public expectations as to the ability of the government to control the economy are naive; they believe that government intervention and tinkering is the problem, not the solution.

> "Practical men, who believe themselves to be quite exempt from any intellectual influences, are usually the slaves of some defunct economist. Madmen in authority, who hear voices in the air, are distilling their frenzy from some academic scribbler of a few years back."
>
> —John Maynard Keynes,
> *The General Theory of Employment Interest and Money* (1936)

At any rate, the most dynamic ideological struggle in macroeconomics today is probably not between capitalism and socialism but between the laissez-faire ideal and corporatist economics, or what some refer to as a *national industrial policy*.

Corporatism, sometimes called *corporativism*, has already influenced the American economy to some degree. Its goal is to minimize conflict in the market and to "coordinate" all aspects of the economy. Corporatists believe in retaining private ownership for the incentive it promotes. However, they also believe in planning to a degree—they say that government should not be a neutral laissez-faire bystander to the economy but should take an active role promoting industry and trade. In their view, government planners should direct both public and private investments into needed sectors with subsidies and technical assistance, such as government-sponsored research. By *coordination*, corporatists mean that government should help guide the interactions of business, labor, education, finance, marketing, and the like so that they cooperate rather than fight each other. The word itself comes from the Latin word *corpus*, meaning "body." The analogy is that the various sectors of the economy should work together much the way the arms, legs, lungs, heart, and eyes of a body work together; each has a function, and none is fully useful without the others. The government's specific role in this body is to act as the coordinating brain.

American corporatists point to Japan's **industrial policy** as model of success. The Japanese Ministry of International Trade and Industry (MITI) focuses the Japanese government's attention, subsidies, tax breaks, direction, assistance, and what it calls *administrative guidance* on particularly important industries—**targeting** them for growth. American corporatists also suggest reforming anti-trust legislation that makes it difficult for American businesses to cooperate with foreign countries that are not hindered in such a way. The first real step in that direction has been the funding of research consortiums, such as the founding in 1987 of *Sematech*. Sematech was originally a five-year project to study semiconducting technology for computer microchips and various other technologies; its goal was to share any findings with all firms that have contributed to its funding. The Pentagon's Defense Advanced Research Projects Agency (DARPA) paid one-half of Sematech's original $250 million budget, and the rest was funded by thirteen high-tech firms that otherwise aggressively compete with each other. Corporatists argue that whereas American businesses are busy fighting each other, Japanese businesses and their government have joined together to outcompete the world. Whereas in 1979 four of the top six computer-chip makers were American (including the top two), by 1990 four of the top six were Japanese (including the top two). Most observers credit Sematech with having reversed this trend, putting U.S. chipmakers in the lead once again in 1993. Its funding for 1992 (Sematech II) was renewed for 5 years at a rate of $200 million per year, split evenly between private corporations and DARPA.

On the other hand, Japan's success has not led to American-style prosperity for the average Japanese. The American standard of living still exceeds that of Japan. About one-third of Japanese houses (most of which are tiny by American standards) do not even have indoor plumbing. (Laissez-faire economists such as Milton Friedman argue that as long as Japan wants to tax its workers in order to subsidize consumer products that we Americans buy from them, we should be happy to receive the benefit!)

Should the U.S. government subsidize research and development of high-definition television (HDTV), as MITI is doing? Within ten years, most American homes will probably have this sharper-image new generation of television. In the late 1980s, American corporatists argued that U.S. firms would not be able to keep up with the Japanese effort if they were not given this assistance, and that the Japanese would monopolize the product. However, as of 1996, after spending more than $10 billion on its analog version of HDTV, it now appears the Japanese have been leapfrogged by unsubsidized American researchers who are developing a digital (computer code) version.

Today most American advocates of an industrial policy are Democrats, although the issue still divides both Democrats and liberals. Some liberals say it is nothing more than "welfare for big business." Most conservatives and Republicans tend to be suspicious of having the government do what the marketplace should do, according to laissez-faire theory. Sematech was an exception to the rule, because it involved research that the Reagan administration considered vital to military technology. However, the Bush administration reversed policy in 1991, agreeing to the establishment of the U.S. Advanced Battery Consortium, in which the Department of Energy will split the $260 million bill with the Detroit Big Three automakers and the electric utility industry. The consortium's research will be primarily devoted to non-polluting electric car technology. Longtime advocates of corporatism, President Clinton and Vice President Gore have initiated projects targeting fuel-efficient cars, a fiber-optic cable "information superhighway," energy-efficient computers, and a number of other high-tech projects involving government-business cooperation. The most costly funding so far has been a $1 billion Pentagon effort to assist AT&T, Xerox, and others in developing flat-panel display screens; the funding was approved by President Clinton in April 1994. (MITI has been funding such research for Sony, Toshiba, and Sharp for some time.)

VARIETIES OF SOCIALISM

In the case of many mixed economies, it is difficult to judge whether the economy is basically capitalist or basically socialist. Instead, some prefer to focus on the trend in certain mixed economies toward more and more elements of socialism (Sweden and the Netherlands are usually cited as examples). This is often called **evolutionary socialism**, which means a gradual, incremental approach to a socialist economy. Specifically, evolutionary socialists advocate a gradual elimination of most private ownership, usually through **nationalization** (public buy-outs of private property and industry), increasing regulation of the market, highly progressive income and corporate taxes (*progressive taxes* tax the rich at higher rates than the poor), and long-term planning of the growth of socialism. Other socialists believe that only the "commanding heights"—that is, the largest elements of the economy (transportation, banking, heavy industry, communications, shipping, etc.)—should be nationalized; the rest should remain private. Sweden is a somewhat unusual case in the sense that very little of the Swedish economy is nationalized—there is very little government ownership of property. However, private businesses are highly regulated in the public interest and are highly taxed to pay for generous cradle-to-grave social benefits. In many Western European governments the socialist parties enact socialist programs when they have a majority in parliament, but when they lose power in a later election many of their programs are overturned. When they regain power the process may repeat itself.

Revolutionary socialists do not want to slowly create socialism through the parliamentary process. They favor a rapid elimination of all private ownership by nationalization, or even **expropriation**: seizure ("by the revolutionary state, in the name of the working class") of all property and capital, with only partial compensation to the owners or none at all. They believe a revolutionary government can and should immediately end the capitalist market and replace it with public ownership and planning. They realize that the transition is difficult and the wealthy will not give in easily to expropriation—which can lead to chaos, violence, or even a civil war. However, they argue that the long-term benefits of socialism outweigh the temporary chaos and conflict of revolution. They also say that the everyday operation of capitalist exploitation of the working-class poor is itself violent.

> "One cannot make an omelet without breaking some eggs."
> —Mao Zedong

Some revolutionary socialists are also *communists*; that is, they believe in the Marxist theory of communism (to be discussed in Chapter 8), in which case they want to quickly create socialism as a stepping stone to eventual communism. The leaders of the Russian revolution (Vladimir Lenin) and the Chinese revolution (Mao Zedong) were communists. However, not all communists are revolutionary; that is, many

Table 5-1		
Economic Systems		

		OWNERSHIP OF PROPERTY	
		private	*public*
	free	laissez-faire capitalism	market socialism
MARKET			
	planned	corporatism	traditional socialism

believe in an evolutionary approach. Communism as an economic system has never existed—not even Communist Party members argue this. However, communists believe that communism will eventually come about, whether through evolution or revolution.

Many of the world's former socialist countries have today abandoned most forms of planning and have privatized much of their property. The remaining socialist countries are experimenting with variations of traditional socialism. So far, the small private enterprises that have been established amount to only a tiny portion of the countries' economies. As for the larger state enterprises, the Soviets began by lessening subsidies and making some of them *self-accounting* or *self-financing*, which means they had to make a profit or go out of business. In the former Yugoslavia, workers owned and managed their own enterprises. As early as the 1960s, Hungarian enterprises—although publicly owned—competed with one another and were relatively independent from state management and planning. This is often called **market socialism**, **reform socialism**, or sometimes *goulash socialism,* after the Hungarian dish. Gorbachev wanted to bring some of the Hungarian-style reforms to the Soviet Union.

CONVERGENCE?

As laissez-faire has been largely abandoned, so has traditional socialism. As early as the 1970s, some commentators argued that socialism and capitalism were slowly but surely merging into one common economic system. It is true that all countries have mixed economies, but advocates of **convergence theory** have believed that practically all distinctions between the Western economic model and the Soviet economic model would eventually blur. In retrospect, it is probably fair to say that the attractiveness of this theory was largely due to the political detente (lessening of tensions) under way between the United States and the Soviet Union. In the late 1970s detente became less popular in the United States, and in the early 1980s the cold war fully re-emerged, which acted to discredit convergence theory. Today, with the end of the cold war, the convergence theory is being resurrected. However, rather than claiming convergence into a single system, it is probably more accurate to say that all countries incorporate elements of each model into their economies, in varying degrees. Although it is fair to say that the U.S. economy reflects some socialist and some corporatist thinking, it is important to note that it is nevertheless overwhelmingly capitalistic.

Key Terms

capitalism
supply and demand
self-interest
socialism
planned economy
command economies
mixed economy
laissez-faire capitalism
modern capitalism

corporatism
industrial policy
targeting
evolutionary socialism
nationalization
revolutionary socialism
expropriation
market socialism/reform socialism
convergence theory

Study Questions

1. What are the fundamental concepts and theories that make up capitalist and socialist ideologies?
2. What are some examples that illustrate the difference between pure ideological theories and the actual practice of economic systems?
3. What are the major arguments for and against both capitalism and socialism?
4. What is a mixed economy? How common is it among countries?
5. What ideological varieties of capitalism and socialism exist, and what are the merits of each?

PART TWO
Ideological Movements

Part Two first discusses the three greatest bodies of Western ideological cal thought: *classical liberalism, classical conservatism,* and *classical socialism.* Next it investigates two challenges to them: *fascism* and *environmentalism.* Each of these five might be best characterized as an ideological movement, because each consists of a large collection of ideological values and theories, and each led to a historic political movement. Part Two ends with a chapter that makes some observations about the *future of ideology.*

CHAPTER 6

CLASSICAL LIBERALISM

THE EMERGENCE OF LIBERALISM

Some historians cite the Magna Charta of 1215, which forced King John of England to guarantee certain fundamental liberties to the people, as the origin of liberalism. In the seventeenth and eighteenth centuries the growth of science and technology, and the concepts of **rationalism** and **progress**, accelerated what is today known as liberal philosophy. Rationalism is the theory that human reasoning and the principles of logic are superior to other bases of knowledge, such as sensory perception, the pronouncements of authorities, spiritual beliefs, and emotionalism. Philosophers argued that just as science offered a method for rational problem-solving in the world of matter and energy, philosophy and reason could be applied to solve social problems and advance human civilization. This notion of progress was a dangerous idea to those who believed the world was as it is because God intended it so. Progress, they believed, was blasphemy. Philosophers who advocated **liberty**—political, social, religious, and economic freedom—as the means of progress were eventually labeled liberals, from the Latin *liber*, which means "free." They suggested that society should be guided by rationalism rather than by the **divine inspiration** (allegedly God-given wisdom) of rulers. In the context of eighteenth-century Europe and its North American colonies, in which liberalism flourished, this was a revolutionary ideology. Historians call this era the **Age of Reason** or (contrasting it with the Dark Ages) the **Enlightenment**.

As suggested above, these philosophers were not called liberals at the time. In 1811 a faction in the Spanish legislature named themselves the *Liberales*. Later, in the 1840s, the British Whigs changed their name to the *Liberals*. Both parties were rooted in the philosophy of the Enlightenment and the Age of Reason, with its emphasis on individual liberty. For this reason, people began to refer to the intellectual predecessors of these parties as liberals. Today we call them *classical liberals*, to differentiate between them and modern liberals.

FEUDAL MONARCHISM

To understand classical liberalism, in which the U.S. Constitution is rooted, one must understand the feudal monarchies against which the classical liberals were rebelling. The root of the word *feudal* is *fief*, which means "fee" and relates to the estate (land, buildings, and peasants) granted to a noble, or vassal. The feudal order, or **feudalism**, was based on the relationship between the monarch (king or queen) and nobles (those with "**noble blood**"—a hereditary elite). Generally, the nobles periodically paid the monarch a fee, or offered military or political service, in return for the monarch's grant of an estate and military protection. The third element of the aristocracy (the elite ruling class) was the clergy. The Church justified the divine right of the king to absolute rule. The serfs, or peasantry, in turn were obliged to serve the nobles by working their land. (There were many variations of the system described here.)

At the time most people were peasants, living in the countryside on the feudal estates. However, a new class of people was slowly emerging, in ever-growing cities. These people were commoners like the peasants, but were free. The economic life of the city was based on the production and trade of manufactured products, many of them new inventions. Mass production of goods for trade was a relatively new phenomenon, which prompted the emergence of craftsmen, artisans, bankers, merchants, traders, shopkeepers—a business class—in the cities. The French word for such a market town was *bourg*, like the German *burg*, or the English *borough*. Thus this class of people would come to be called the **bourgeoisie** ("boor-zhwa-ze"). The nobles strictly regulated the economic activities of the bourgeoisie and heavily taxed their profits.

The liberal movement was made up of philosophers from all over Europe, but especially France and Britain. These philosophers included

Hobbes, Voltaire, Rousseau, Descartes, Montesquieu, Locke, and many others. In America some of the most prominent were Jefferson, Madison, Paine, and Franklin, each of whom was quite familiar with the above-mentioned European philosophers. To a large extent, these liberal philosophers represented the interests of the emerging middle-class bourgeoisie, who agreed with them that the feudal monarchies were unjust and inefficient. Liberals criticized feudalism on many fronts: political, social, religious, and economic.

POLITICAL LIBERTY

Politically, only a privileged few held any power, and that power was absolute or nearly so. Many liberals viewed government as little better than a necessary evil; that is, government by its very nature infringes upon human freedom, but without it lies chaos. Therefore, the task was how to make a government system that promoted security, stability, and social order without sacrificing freedom and individualism. The liberals' answer was **constitutionalism**; that is, limited, restrained government. The primary means of limiting government was through the **separation of power** into three branches, such as was suggested by John Locke in *Two Treatises on Civil Government* (1690) and Charles de Montesquieu in *The Spirit of the Laws* (1734). Separation of powers was an ancient theoretical concept, but Locke and Montesquieu popularized it among liberals.

> "If men were angels, there would be no need for government."
> —The *Federalist* Papers

Power was not to be divided cleanly between the three branches. Rather, there would be overlapping jurisdictions, which would result in competition among the branches of government. This is called **checks and balances**: the mechanism through which each branch of government prevents the other two from exercising inordinate power. Government must reflect human nature, and human nature is self-interested. Without checks and balances, individuals would take too much power and become corrupted because of it.

Also crucial to the concept of constitutional government is political restraint—the idea that a government must be bound by fundamental laws that protect the people's civil liberties from government power. John Locke wrote of **natural rights**—"life, liberty, and property," which no government could justifiably take away from the people. Locke insisted that government does not, and cannot, grant the people such rights—

they are born with them. The people create and empower government to protect these rights. According to Thomas Hobbes, and later Jean-Jacques Rousseau, the people voluntarily enter into a **social contract** with their government, which is bound to honor these natural rights. The Founding Fathers spelled out this contract through the U.S. Constitution. Similarly, Thomas Jefferson used the term *unalienable rights* in the Declaration of Independence, although he described them as including "life, liberty, and the pursuit of happiness." (However, the Fifth Amendment to the U.S. Constitution is worded to protect "life, liberty, [and] property.")

> "The only purpose for which power can be rightfully exercised over any member of a civilized community, against his will, is to prevent harm to others. His own good, either physical or moral, is not sufficient warrant."
>
> —John Stuart Mill

Liberals argued that the natural rights of an individual cannot be limited by government, although individuals must honor certain obligations to society as a part of the social contract. Rather, individual rights are limited only to the extent that they infringe on another individual's rights. This means that individual discretion in private matters should be highly protected, even if the majority considers a behavior unorthodox or damaging to the individual. Individualism in social interactions should be restricted only if it threatens to harm others.

> "The enumeration in the Constitution, of certain rights, shall not be construed to deny or disparage others retained by the people."
> —Ninth Amendment, U.S. Constitution

Many of the federalists who wrote the U.S. Constitution thought it "dangerous" to include a specific list of civil liberties (a bill of rights) in the Constitution. They felt that government could not grant natural rights—after all, they are inalienable. The federal Constitution was severely limited and had no authority to infringe on the citizens' liberty. Further, some might claim that a list of civil liberties would constitute a complete list of rights, and anything not listed therein could be assumed excluded. Because of this concern, the Ninth Amendment was added to the Constitution.

SOCIAL LIBERTY

Prior to the liberal movement, most philosophers accepted the idea that individuals were born into a social class. They were born with or without talents to be a ruler, soldier, artisan, or farmer. Only those of noble breeding were fit to rule others. Only they were able to judge good and evil, and only they had the moral character to lead. In this view, societies that allowed commoners to participate in governance were destined to ruin.

Most liberals challenged the social inequities of their day. Rousseau championed the dignity and worth of common people, arguing that they had the right to reject their rulers and illegitimate laws to which they had not consented. American liberals in particular spurned the rigid class structure of Europe. In fact, the U.S. Constitution forbids the government's granting of a "Title of Nobility." There was no chance for social mobility in feudal society. Those masses of people unfortunate enough to be born into serfdom were practically enslaved to their feudal lords, the noblemen—although on rare occasions some serfs were freed or escaped to the cities. And no matter how successful a bourgeois merchant was, he would never have "noble blood." Neither serf nor merchant could ever rise to the ruling class; aristocrats got their position by birth, not merit.

Some of the most elegant words ever penned on the subject of equality were penned by Thomas Jefferson in the Declaration of Independence: "We hold these truths to be self-evident, that all men are created equal . . ." Yet Jefferson, like most of the Founding Fathers, was a slaveholder. These men did not advocate social equality, freedom, and mobility of the kind Americans know today. Although a few of them advocated the abolition of slavery and the institution of voting rights for women, most did not. However, they were relatively egalitarian for the time in which they lived.

RELIGIOUS LIBERTY

As for religious freedom, the clergy enforced strict obedience to its Church and intimidated the peasantry into passivity. To be disloyal to the monarch (or nobles) was considered to be disloyal to God, since the monarch was divinely ordained. The monarch was said to be a descendent of the family God had chosen to rule, and thus had a **divine right** to govern. For this reason, liberals often viewed the clergy as the monarch's instrument of repression. At a minimum, the clergy and the monarch cooperated to enforce conformity and stifle any unorthodox views that threatened authority. The Spanish Liberales, mentioned previ-

ously, argued for the adoption of a new constitution similar to the radical (liberal) 1791 French constitution, which the monarchists and Catholic
Church condemned as religious and philosophical heresy. In the U.S.
Constitution, the Founding Fathers guaranteed religious freedom and
prohibited the establishment of a state religion or the use of religious
tests as a requirement for public officeholders.

Although some of the liberals were atheists, most were very religious
men. They were condemned by conservatives and religious authorities
not because of the words of a few of them, but because their ideology
threatened the power of the clergy and offered secular (nonreligious, not
anti-religious) guidance to society. Because the state religion was such a
powerful component of feudal monarchism, the attack on monarchism
undermined the clergy's authority. The liberals' rationalism provided an
alternative to religious interpretation of government, traditional authorities, fanaticism, and superstition.

ECONOMIC LIBERTY

Just as important as (some say much more important than) their political,
social, and religious agenda was the liberals' demand for economic freedom. They criticized feudalism for its economic inefficiency. The prime
argument was the lack of incentive caused by the smothering control of
the nobles over the market. The harder the bourgeoisie worked, the more
the nobles taxed them. Entrance into professions was strictly regulated,
marketplaces were controlled, foreign trade was restricted, and so on.
The bourgeoisie viewed the nobles as little better than inbred leeches
and hated them for the stifling taxes they imposed. And as for the serfs,
no degree of hard work could ever change their position in society.

Even worse than taxes was the outright theft of property by the
nobility. The lack of substantial and enforceable **property rights** meant
that the bourgeoisie's property was never really secure from seizure (or
at least control) by the aristocracy. Therefore, just as important as the
social contract was to political liberty and constitutionalism, the notions
of **contract law** and property rights were vital to economic liberty. One
of the primary reasons for government, after all, is the protection of
property rights. Liberals believed that individuals should be protected by
economic contracts just as they are protected by the *political contract*
that bounds their government. Although the Fifth Amendment to the U.S.
Constitution does not grant absolute property rights, it does guarantee
that individuals may not be deprived of their property "without due
process of law; nor shall private property be taken for public use, without just compensation."

The Scottish liberal Adam Smith laid the philosophical foundations of laissez-faire capitalism. In his famous book, *The Wealth of Nations* (1776), he argued that the individual's pursuit of economic self-interest is the life-blood of a successful economy. The lure of limitless profit provides incentive to work hard and a motivation to take risks by investing **capital** (money, property). As the individual profits, he accumulates even more capital; capital accumulation in turn leads to investment. Investments in new enterprises open new jobs for the working class and further expand the economy. The profits of the capitalist therefore eventually reach even the poorest members of society; thus free enterprise benefits all. (Will Rogers, a Depression-era political satirist, first derisively titled this notion the **trickle-down theory**, implying that only a trickle actually reaches the lower classes.)

According to Smith, because self-interest promotes the economic well-being of everyone, it is a much better instrument of economic growth and prosperity than is a monarch's iron hand. Without a ruler or government to intervene and smother initiative and progress, self-interest would act as an **invisible hand**, guiding the market in the most productive, efficient way. It would be "invisible" because there would be no noticeable coercive force (a government) present to hold back the individual; however, a guiding "hand" is in fact present—the market's laws of *supply and demand*. To make profits, the investor has only to obey the wishes of the market; that is, he has to judge what is in demand and quickly produce and market it. Furthermore, his product must be of good quality because of the fierce competition in the market. If the capitalist does not respond quickly, efficiently, and with high quality and reasonable prices, the market will weed out the capitalist.

The appeal of Smith's analysis is at least in part due to the notion that society can be improved without the necessity of social cooperation by masses of individuals. Rather, social betterment occurs naturally, regardless of the intent of individuals, because their natural competitiveness is allowed to freely act.

> "It is not from the benevolence of the butcher, the brewer, or the baker that we expect our dinner, but from their regard to their own interest."
> —Adam Smith

In terms of foreign trade, Smith attacked what he called **mercantilism**, the economic policy that European governments had practiced (against each other) since the sixteenth century. The goal of this policy was a favorable balance of trade through an aggressive export policy coupled with restraints on imports. The trade surplus would result in gold and silver transfers by the importing countries (especially overseas colonies) to the exporting countries. It also entailed many arbitrary and counterproductive regulations that had been enacted not out of concern for the national interest but by powerful merchants (the "shopkeepers," as Smith sarcastically called them). Most economically counterproductive was the granting of monopoly status to certain companies in their trade with the colonies. Smith argued that accumulation of precious metals was not an accurate measure of "the wealth of nations," and that restrictions on free trade hurt all countries, not just those whose exports were being restricted.

Smith influenced later economists such as David Ricardo, who argued that all countries should specialize in their **comparative advantage**: the products they can most efficiently produce in comparison to other countries. Every country has a comparative advantage—even if it is not the most efficient producer in the world of any product, there will always be certain products that it produces better than other products. (In such cases, there will be certain products in which the country is at the *least disadvantage* as compared to other countries.) Profits a country earns from exports of its comparative advantage–product can be used to pay for imports that it would otherwise inefficiently produce. Free trade benefits countries just as free trade benefits individuals, who prosper by specializing in their skill and buying other products with their earnings. Of course, there is resistance to free trade by "shopkeepers" and the employees of businesses that are producing products in which the country has no comparative advantage, because international competition would destroy them. Competition, however, is the natural force (the invisible hand) that pushes individuals into advantageous markets where they profit even more. Smith and Ricardo attributed mercantilist policies to the political power of those who had a poor understanding of economics.

After the ratification in 1789 of the U.S. Constitution, which prohibited tariffs and other trade barriers between the states, the American national economy grew quickly as each state began to specialize in its comparative advantages and traded its products for those of the other states.

CLASSICAL LIBERALS AND MODERN LIBERALS

The arguments of the classical liberals implied great changes for society, so the word *liberal* also became associated with the proponents of change, or progress, a connotation that still holds today. Like classical liberals, modern liberals still fight conservatives over issues concerning the limits of individual freedom. Conservatives, whether those of modern times or *classical conservatives* of the seventeenth and eighteenth centuries, tend(ed) to support the status quo—or at least moderate reform rather than radical changes.

Early twentieth-century progressives were occasionally called *liberal*, but the term was not widely used in the United States until Franklin Roosevelt championed it, beginning in his first presidential election campaign in 1932. Since Roosevelt's party—the Democrats—was the minority party, he needed a "progressive"-sounding symbolic label that could attract the Progressive wing of the Republican Party. The most likely reason Roosevelt adopted the liberal label is his general agreement with the principles of the British Liberal Party, which shared common ideological ground with Roosevelt's plans (specifically his New Deal program). By the 1930s, British Liberals were charting a middle course between socialism and laissez-faire capitalism. The British Liberal economist John Maynard Keynes wrote of "controlling and directing economic forces in the interests of social justice and social stability," an attractive suggestion during the Great Depression. Roosevelt knew that the voters would support the notion of an active government pursuing economic reform. This label might also deflect criticisms of his economic ideology and claims that he was a socialist. Thus the American definition of the word *liberal* was determined more by the British party label than by the classical liberal movement, although the British Liberal Party itself descended from classical liberalism.

Just as the classical liberals wanted limitations on the political power of government, an end to social immobility, and freedom of religion, they wanted a "government that governs least" in the marketplace as well. Given the laissez-faire economic philosophy of the classical liberals, the reader may wonder why British Liberals such as Keynes advocated government regulation of the economy, something Adam Smith would certainly oppose. The simple answer is that Smith did not live in the age of industrial capitalism and its associated ills. The gap between classical liberals and modern liberals was bridged by liberal philosophers such as John Stuart Mill, who warned that great concentrations of property by capitalists (at the expense of their employees) contradicted individual liberty and social equality.

For Keynes, the alternatives were the Labour Party, which he considered a socialist party that did not respect property rights at all, and the Conservative Party, which offered no ideas for change. The Conservatives continued to preach laissez-faire capitalism even though in the eyes of the British Liberals it had condemned many people to poverty and inequality. The Liberals believed that in order to further advance the cause of freedom, they would have to adjust their economic philosophy to reconcile it with their political and social conceptions of individual liberty. Roosevelt answered his critics by saying that by making small reforms in capitalism, he was saving it from revolutionary socialism.

Conservatives, then and now, point out that modern liberalism has strayed from classical liberalism's economic philosophy. In fact, in terms of their economic values the classical liberals have more in common with modern (laissez-faire) conservatives—both oppose(ed) government interference in the market. Of course, they are products of different eras. Liberals, both then and now, support(ed) economic change—classical liberals wanted to create capitalism, and modern liberals want to reform or manage capitalism.

Key Terms

rationalism	natural rights
progress	social contract
Age of Reason/Enlightenment	divine right
liberty	property rights
divine inspiration	contract law
feudalism	capital
noble blood	trickle-down theory
bourgeoisie	invisible hand
constitutionalism	mercantilism
separation of power	comparative advantage
checks and balances	

Study Questions

1. What is the origin of the term *liberal*, and how was it introduced into the modern American political vocabulary?
2. What is the difference between classical liberals and modern American liberals?
3. What was the agenda of the classical liberals?
4. In what historical context was classical liberalism born?
5. How did classical liberalism shape the U.S. Constitution and political system?

CHAPTER 7

CLASSICAL CONSERVATISM

CLASSICAL CONSERVATISM VERSUS CLASSICAL LIBERALISM

The rise of classical liberalism was matched with the rise of what we today call *classical conservatism*. Conservative thought acted as a counterweight to liberal movement. If the classical socialist movement was the left-wing response to liberalism, the classical conservative movement was the right-wing reaction. Each helped temper liberalism and define it as a moderate ideological movement.

   With classical liberalism in mind, and considering what the liberals were in rebellion against, it is tempting to think conservatives supported and wanted to "conserve" feudal monarchism and opposed the liberals' ideas about freedom, constitutionalism, capitalism, and so on. This is not entirely true. They agreed with the liberals on many points and shared a common vocabulary and many common assumptions. In fact, scholars sometimes disagree as to whether certain philosophers were liberals or conservatives. The difference, simply put, is the same basic difference between modern liberals and conservatives: disagreement about the pace and extent of change. They both participated in the philosophical revolution known today as the Enlightenment. However, the conservatives did not share the liberals' optimism about the ability of human reason alone (rationalism)—without the aid of centuries of accumulated experience, knowledge, culture, and tradition—to conquer social ills and create a better world.

> "There are no longer any priests; they have been exiled, slaughtered, and debased. . . . those who escaped the guillotine, the stake, daggers, fusillades, drownings, and deportation today receive the alms that formerly they themselves gave. You feared the force of custom, the ascendancy of authority. . . . None of these things are left; man's mind is his own. Philosophy [author's note: liberalism, rationalism] having corroded the cement that united men, there are no longer any moral bonds."
>
> —Joseph De Maistre,
> *Considerations on France* (1797),
> translated by Richard A. Lebrun

The clearest example of the danger posed by liberalism was the French Revolution. Although it began with laudable liberal ideals of "liberty, equality, and fraternity," it quickly degenerated into a bloody "reign of terror" not only against the nobility and clergy but even among the revolutionaries themselves. It was marked by the abolition of feudalism, mob violence, great instability in government, economic chaos, wars with France's neighbors, severe restrictions on the power of the Catholic Church, and a repudiation of almost every institution and source of order and authority the conservatives cherished.

Two of the most prominent classical conservatives were the great British politician Edmund Burke and the French emigré Joseph De Maistre. Burke attacked the French Revolution in his famous *Reflections on the Revolution in France* (1790). Burke was most concerned about the reckless destruction of institutions, order, and stability. He saw a country taken over by inexperienced, insolent, illiterate, unprincipled "clowns" who gave themselves unlimited power with no established laws, rules, procedures, or restraints. Because he wrote in 1790, before most of the horrific mob violence and the "reign of terror" had occurred, his ideas seemed almost prophetic. De Maistre's *Considerations on France* followed in 1797, eight years into the revolution. De Maistre, who (unlike Burke) was a French Catholic, was particularly enraged by what he believed was the anti-religious character of the "satanic" revolution, although he too was concerned about the general disintegration of social order owing to rapid changes. Like all classical conservatives, he considered the mass public unsophisticated and easily deceived by democratic demagogues who had no sense of virtue and wisdom. The so-called

French Republic was little more than "the feverish discussions and drunken revels of an unbridled populace." According to De Maistre, France's turmoil was God's punishment for the rise of liberalism and revolution in France. He called for the restoration of the monarchy and the clergy. Burke and De Maistre did much to unite and define conservatism.

ORGANICISM

Clearly, classical liberalism triumphed over classical conservatism in the Western world, but classical conservatism made its contribution as well and did not wither away as an ideology. It is best represented today by the organic conservatives described in Chapter 2. These modern conservatives take their metaphorical label from the classical conservative view of society as a single living organism, rather than a collection of individuals. This **organicism** is the greatest difference they had with liberals, who were extremely individualistic.

Classical conservatives believed individuals had natural rights—but in the context of what society determined, not what they individually demanded. Individualistic interpretations of natural rights and liberty lead to anarchy and immorality. Most conservatives believed order was more important than liberty; at a minimum there must be a careful balance between the two, sometimes called *regulated liberty* or *ordered liberty*. In this view, social order, stability, and security are just as important to individuals as is liberty. In fact, they are arguably more immediate and basic needs than freedom is. Moreover, rights entail duties; one cannot exist without the other. The social contract is not a one-way street; because individuals benefit from society, they are obligated to repay society by protecting and preserving it. It is a debt to prior generations and generations to come; to avoid it is immoral.

> "The only liberty I mean, is a liberty connected with order; that not only exists along with order and virtue, but which cannot exist at all without them."
>
> —Edmund Burke

To a modern-day American, it may seem self-evident that individual rights should be paramount. As the liberal John Stuart Mill put it: "The worth of a State, in the long run, is the worth of the individuals composing it." Classical conservatives like Burke would not necessarily dispute Mill's assertion, since individuals may contribute to society in either an evil manner or a virtuous manner. However, they would consider this formula incomplete, because they view society as much greater than the sum of its individuals. It consists of groups, families, neighbors, nations, classes, institutions, moral codes, tradition, heritage, religion, customs, and accumulated wisdom, all of which fit together in one complex living being we call society. As Burke argued, the dynamic sum of all of these relationships, delicately interwoven with each other, constitutes the **social fabric**. Conservatives believed liberals exaggerated the importance of individuals to the exclusion of consideration of the society and its enduring relationships and institutions. This does not mean they were disinterested in people—individuals must live in society, and society largely shapes its individuals' happiness and fulfillment. The French Revolution, according to Burke, had torn the social fabric and reduced a people into "vague, loose individuals," just as a tear in cloth can eventually reduce it to a pile of threads.

> "Individuals pass like shadows; but the commonwealth is fixed and stable."
>
> —Edmund Burke

Society consists of many intricate relationships, established gradually over many years of political, economic, and social evolution. Like a body, its parts are interdependent. Tinkering with its normal operations through poorly designed reform is like experimental surgery at best. Change is natural, if slowly and steadily enacted, like the normal growth of a living thing. Burke called this kind of change **reform**. However, **innovation** and improvement for its sake alone is similar to cosmetic surgery with its later unintended and unpredicted consequences. In other words, radical change unhinges public order, stability, and security and threatens to unleash more problems than it solves, because those who meddle in society rarely understand how all parts fit together. The conservatives offered a healthy dose of skepticism to liberals and socialists, whom the conservatives saw as intoxicated with ideas about changing the world. Yes, government should reform society, when absolutely necessary—but not eagerly, whenever possible.

> "The Huichol Indians believe perfection is only done by God, so when they put beads on their [artistic figures] they always intentionally put on one of the wrong color, an intentional imperfection called *el toque Huichol*, the Huichol touch."
>
> —*Trade and Culture*, Fall 1993, p. 38.

IRRATIONALISM

The classical conservatives did not enthusiastically embrace rationalism and can be called **irrationalists**, or *anti-rationalists*. They argued that human society and nature are infinitely complex and beyond the realm of rationalization. To pretend to understand how society functions when social science only superficially explains some of its isolated parts is absurd. As irrationalists, the conservatives did not reject human reason. Rather, they insisted it be balanced by tradition, custom, religious revelation, and accumulated wisdom.

Irrationalism has been reinforced today by **chaos theory**. Some modern mathematicians and physicists have theorized that the natural world is fundamentally irregular and unpredictable. Its component parts are not only too numerous to identify but have infinite interconnections and relationships with one another. The millions of unrecognized interactions and uncatalogued phenomena influence larger factors that in turn affect still greater factors, making it fundamentally impossible to predict the behavior of the natural world. At a minimum, the recognition of chaos is humbling to scientists who dream of human mastery of the laws of nature. At a maximum, it lends great credibility to the irrationalists. After all, if the natural world is so unpredictable, how much more difficult is it to diagnose and prescribe cures for social ills?

THE NATURAL ARISTOCRACY

Like the liberals, most classical conservatives believed government should be limited through constitutionalism. However, a constitution was not just a document derived through reason. It was experience and tradition according to Burke, and divine inspiration according to De Maistre. Both also argued against what would today be considered a legalistic or strict interpretation of written constitutionality, which would preclude the enlightened ruler from doing what was right. Furthermore, they were not opposed to monarchism and did not share the liberals' distrust of the state. Conservatives argued that the state should be led by a virtuous, civilized, **natural aristocracy**. Thomas Jefferson also advocated a "natural aristocracy," but he truly meant a *meritocracy*, an aristocracy based on merit, whereas Burke and De Maistre specifically endorsed a *hereditary monarchy*. To be fair, both assumed that a hereditary aristocracy was natural because the nobility, being wealthy men of leisure, had the time to read and learn manners and discipline, and were able to see the general society's interest over the narrow interests of individuals. These wise men must educate their citizens, in an effort to build a virtuous society based on responsibility and cooperation. In this view, the liberals' obsession with equality and democracy is unnatural and destabilizing.

> "A perfect democracy is therefore the most shameless thing in the world."
>
> —Edmund Burke

PROPERTY

Conservatives also supported the notion of private property, but for different reasons than the liberals. Liberals viewed property as an end unto itself—a reward for enterprise, and a natural right. Conservatives believed in property because it created a desirable social good. "Men of property" would be better citizens, because they have a real investment in society, or something to protect and defend against changes. Owners of property are more likely to see their well-being as intrinsically tied to society's well-being, which is how it truly is. Conservatives also disagreed with the liberals' worship of contract law, which implies no permanent, fundamental standards beyond what individuals agree to at the time. In this view, contracts should not be considered a complete list of obligations. Ownership of property, like liberty, comes with certain duties to the community. Property must be used responsibly. The private marketplace, and rational (self-interested) behavior, do not always ensure wise use of property; the invisible hand is no panacea.

THE AMERICAN REVOLUTION

It was clear to liberals and conservatives alike that the American Revolution was quite different from the French Revolution. It resulted in thirteen independent states rather than one. The U.S. Constitution separated powers and created strong checks and balances. It was led almost entirely by cautious, well-educated elites with little involvement by commoners. Religious and cultural diversity already existed in the country. There was no nobility, and the king was far away across the ocean.

Nevertheless, although Burke was quite favorable to American independence, most classical conservatives were pessimistic. De Maistre doubted the stability of the American government and claimed in *Considerations on France* the odds were "a thousand to one" that the city of Washington would never be built and no Congress would ever meet there. He believed that one of the reasons for the Americans' foolhardy rebellion against their king across the ocean was the fact that they never got to see the "splendour of monarchy." He ridiculed the Americans' constitution-building as a "chimerical system of deliberation and political construction by abstract reasoning"—instead of the accumulated wisdom of the centuries. (A *chimera* is a mythological monster made up of various parts from different species—a Frankenstein, more or less, rather than a naturally grown *organism*.)

Although Burke was unusually republican as compared to other classical conservatives, he is today the best-known and archetypal conservative. This is probably because he had more in common with liberals than other classical conservatives. De Maistre and a variety of other German conservatives, aristocrats from all over Europe, and papal authorities were labeled **the Reaction** (reactionaries). They were never as popular as Burke, whose ideas live on among organic conservatives.

Key Terms

organicism

social fabric

innovation versus reform (Burkean)

irrationalism

chaos theory

natural aristocracy

the Reaction

Study Questions

1. What is the difference between classical liberalism and classical conservatism, particularly concerning rationalism, organicism, individualism, constitutionalism, and property?
2. How did the French Revolution mobilize classical conservatism?
3. What is the difference between conservatives like Burke and those like De Maistre?
4. How does the classical conservative's view of liberty compare with that of the classical liberal? Compare Burke's view of liberty with that of Benjamin Franklin's: "The citizen that tolerates oppression in the name of security deserves neither liberty nor security."
5. What differences between the American and French revolutions would account for Burke's pessimism about one and optimism about the other?

CHAPTER 8

CLASSICAL SOCIALISM

EARLY SOCIALISM

Various Greek and Roman philosophers promoted communal sharing of society's property, as well as its responsibilities, as the path to a virtuous society. However, they typically excluded the majority of the people from their "society." Therefore, some argue that the first true socialists were the early Christians. Christianity offered revolutionary ideals of egalitarianism and communalism, suggesting that all people were equal in the eyes of God and that each had a duty to help the poor and the suffering. Many religious thinkers argued that greed and envy were sins fostered by inequality, and left people morally corrupted. In 1519 the Englishman Sir Thomas More (later canonized as a martyr by the Catholic Church) wrote *Utopia*, a novel about a future society in which private property and money are abolished and poverty and hunger are ended.

In the early nineteenth century, European socialists, such as Charles Fourier and Robert Owen, advocated small-scale socialist **communes** in which the inhabitants would freely contribute their work and collectively share goods. (Such communes were in fact established in many countries, including the United States, although most failed.) Whereas Fourier was mainly a dreamer, Owen, a wealthy businessman, put his money where his mouth was, designing and operating a progressive model factory, building a commune, and advocating worker-owned cooperatives as a building block to a decentralized socialistic society. Other early nineteenth-century socialists advocated a more centralized version. Henri de Saint-Simon was the first to write about planning, as a more productive and efficient economic system managed by scientists rather than by random market forces—as was laissez-faire capitalism.

CRITICISM OF LAISSEZ-FAIRE CAPITALISM

Generally speaking, classical liberalism's democratic ideals of political, social, and religious freedom continued to spread around the world during the nineteenth century. In terms of philosophy, liberalism's rationalism triumphed over tradition and superstition. However, during this same time there arose a growing storm of criticism concerning laissez-faire capitalism as it had developed.

Capitalist ideologues were fascinated with Charles Darwin's 1859 work, *Origin of Species*, which explained his theory of natural selection (commonly known as "survival of the fittest"). In a nutshell, Darwin said that competition in nature eliminates weaker organisms from the gene pool and therefore favors the occasional genetic mutation that happens to make the organism stronger, or more adaptable. This is the driving force behind evolution, which improves the species. Some transferred what Darwin had written about nature to society; these people were called **social Darwinists**. By this logic, competition in the marketplace was akin to competition in "the jungle" or nature. What this implies is that by interfering in the marketplace, government ultimately weakens the human species—the *natural* law of survival of the fittest is not allowed to operate. At the time, this was a particularly compelling argument, because it sounded scientific. In the nineteenth century, (classical) liberals (and Marxists as well) claimed to be applying science to ideology, rationalizing it. *International social Darwinists* applied Darwin's theory to the jungle of international conflict, saying that the fittest nations should survive. This idea contributed to fascism and justified war against "weaker and inferior" nations.

Critics argued that social Darwinism ignored the fact that society does not operate as does nature—that in fact separation from the natural world is the very essence of social organization. That is, if the free market were truly a "jungle," there would exist no police, courts, or laws to protect capital accumulation and private property. The capitalist would be overcome by hungry competitors, as would be any animal in the jungle. Furthermore, most capitalists did not competitively struggle to earn their wealth through hard work, as the writer Horatio Alger implied. Instead, they acquired it the old-fashioned way: they inherited it. Still other socialists attacked social Darwinism on humanistic grounds, insisting that humans are not savage animals and are indeed capable of rising above natural selfishness and brutality.

No doubt the American socialist Upton Sinclair had social Darwinism in mind when he titled his 1905 book *The Jungle*, in which he described the terrible conditions of the working class under industrial capitalism. It appeared to many that *incentive* had become completely barbaric—workers labored as many as 90 hours per week, while their children (who also worked) died of disease or malnutrition. They worked hard—not "to get ahead," which was almost impossible, but because of the threat of unemployment; there was always someone else available to take their place, should they appear to be a "troublemaker." Workers also feared losing their jobs because they were aware of the *boom and bust* cyclical nature of the unregulated economy. Even the best workers lost their jobs in the recurring recessions. To a worker without a job, natural selection became more than just a theory, because there were no government assistance programs.

Besides incentive, another key concept to capitalism—*competition*—came under attack. Classical liberals, such as Adam Smith, had never imagined the rise of huge corporations that managed to destroy all competitors and monopolize a particular market. Socialists claimed there was no real competition in the leading national industries. Even in large markets, where there were several great competitors, they were accused of fixing prices and acting as a cartel.

Finally, socialists demanded a more egalitarian distribution of wealth. Regardless of the theory, *trickle-down* simply did not work to the satisfaction of the poor. At the same time the unemployed were starving, the rich were conspicuously consuming. According to socialists, this was not just a question of economics but of democracy itself.

The abuses and excesses of laissez-faire capitalism ultimately led to three separate results. In the United States, for example, they led to a great labor movement, which slowly won reforms that improved working conditions and raised the standard of living. Social Security and eventually a myriad of welfare programs were born. And since the Depression, the government has taken an active role in regulating the economy in an attempt to stabilize and promote it. These reforms, many of which were originally advocated by "radicals" (as socialists and communists were generally called), were enacted by Democrats and Republicans—who thereby "stole the fire" of the American socialist movement to a great degree.

In other countries, socialists had even more success. In addition to such reforms, socialist parties have become active partners in government and have nationalized much of their countries' leading industries. They have promoted a more highly mixed economy than that of the United States. Most European countries fit into this category.

In the Russian empire, the result was the overthrow of the government in 1917 and the eventual establishment of the first revolutionary socialist state, the Soviet Union. The announced goal of the revolutionary Bolshevik Party was *communism*. In fact, in 1918 the Bolsheviks changed their party name to the Communist Party. But before we can discuss communism, we must first study the body of ideological thought known as Marxism.

MARXISM

Whereas classical liberalism was a revolutionary ideology in the feudal order, **Marxism** arose as a revolutionary ideology in capitalist society. A great many philosophers contributed to one or more separate components of liberalism; a study of only one of these writers cannot define the totality of liberalism. However, socialist ideology became a powerful and revolutionary force owing largely to one German philosopher—Karl Marx. Scholars debate whether Marx was primarily a revolutionary ideologue or a social scientist. He participated in a number of radical political organizations and appealed to the working class to unite in rebellion against their exploiters. On the other hand, he thought of himself as a social scientist rather than an ideologue. That is, he believed he was describing what *is* (and *was* and *would be*) rather than what *should be*. Most philosophers consider his prophesies *deterministic*; that is, Marx wrote of an inevitable course of history that could not be substantially altered or forestalled by political movements. According to his colleague Friedrich Engels, near the end of Marx's life, when many began calling themselves "Marxists," he answered: "All I know is I am not a Marxist." Marx and others labeled most early socialist philosophers, whom Marx believed were ideological rather than scientific, as **utopians**. The label *utopian socialism* is thought to have originated from More's novel *Utopia*, mentioned above. Marxism represented the combination of the utopian socialist spirit with the Enlightenment's rationalism.

With Engels's help, Marx created a theory of human history based on the philosophical principles of dialectics and materialism. **Dialectics** refers to an analytical process of reconciling two equally compelling arguments—the *thesis* and the *antithesis*. These "two sides of the same coin" are mutually contradictory, yet each depends on one another for its meaning, just as there cannot be only one side of a coin. Good cannot be understood without the concept of evil. Positive is meaningless without negative. A higher level of "truth" can be found in combining, or reconciling, both the thesis and antithesis—into a *synthesis*. The synthesis then becomes the new dominant argument, the thesis, which prompts the emergence of an antithesis, and the process repeats itself. Marx compared these two sides to social classes—those with power and those without. The synthesis is represented by revolution, which rearranges class structures and produces a new dominant class (thesis). Dialectics assumes this process of historical change is progressive, toward increasingly superior (efficient, just, harmonious, prosperous, peaceful, fulfilling, etc.) societies.

Materialism implies a rejection of mysticism and a focus on the real, tangible, verifiable world. In simplified terms, materialism rejected many of the popular explanations for history, such as "the winds of fate," personalities of rulers, religion, ideology, and the like. According to Marx, historical change is driven by materialism, specifically the **class struggle**—the dialectical conflict between the dominant (ruling) class and the subservient, exploited classes.

Marx also used the concept of materialism to reject popular ways of defining and categorizing societies, such as by the nature of their social or political order, their religion, their educational system, their legal system, or their architecture. Marx said that these characteristics, albeit important, do not define a society, as does its economic system. (This was quite similar to Saint-Simon's explanation of human history, divided into stages of economic development.) Marx's theory of **economic determinism** held that the mode of production, trade, and consumption in a society will determine all other aspects of that society—not vice versa, as other writers claimed. Therefore, in order to chart historical stages (eras), Marx classified societies according to their means of production. In this view, the economic system determines the class structure, and the class struggle is the driving force in historical change.

Pre-Feudal Economies

Marx said that tribal societies, with simple hunter-gatherer economies, were originally classless. (For this reason, he occasionally referred to tribalism as *primitive communism*.) Owing to competition for land and resources, tribes grew, conquered one another, and developed classes: namely, citizens and slaves. Meanwhile, the birth of agriculture and farming tools (materialist changes) created surpluses of food, which required decisions as to how it was divided, traded, stored, and protected. This created leadership positions and even more class distinctions. Marx referred to this order as *ancient communalism*. Once classes emerge, the state (government) emerges, and the dominant class uses the state to exploit the other classes. Marx said the state is the "tool of the dominant class." Because of efficiency of size and growing socioeconomic stratification, feudalism emerged.

Feudalism

In feudal societies there were three main classes: the aristocracy (monarch, nobles, and clergy), the peasantry (serfs or slaves), and later, the bourgeoisie. As the bourgeoisie grew in numbers (with the growth of technology and the advent of private property), they became more and more class-conscious of their exploitation at the hands of the aristocracy, who taxed and controlled them. Eventually, the bourgeoisie in many European countries overthrew the dominant class of aristocrats and seized state power for themselves, becoming the new dominant class.

Capitalism

Under capitalism, a new class emerged: the **proletariat**, or the working class. The bourgeoisie were no longer the middle class; they were the new dominant class, exploiting the labor of the proletariat and the peasantry. The proletariat grew as industry grew and the peasantry left the farms for the industrial cities. Marx said the working class is exploited for its labor. The profit generated by **surplus value** (labor that the worker is not paid for) is the means of the capitalist's exploitation. The bourgeois class is able to exploit the workers' labor because it controls the state and uses it to justify private ownership of the means of production, just as the nobles used the state to justify their ownership of the land and control of the markets. Through their control of the state, the bourgeoisie control education and socialization, inducing a **false consciousness** that causes the proletariat to support the very social and political institutions that exploit them.

At the same time, the industrial economy **alienates** the individual from his or her true identity as a thinking human. The capitalist mode of production reduces the typical worker to involuntary, ritualistic, noncreative labor. The worker does not theorize and then creatively act on his or her vision; rather, the worker responds to commands and follows established, bureaucratized procedures and is thus separated from what it means to be uniquely human.

According to Marx, capitalism inexorably moves to more and more "efficient" stages, with the capitalists continually trying to maximize profits. To do this, the capitalist must maximize surplus value. Because of competition, the capitalists that best accomplish this will survive, defeating their competitors; therefore, the tendency will necessarily be toward minimizing the amount paid to the proletariat and, when possible, eliminating their jobs altogether, through greater productivity and mechanization of production. Capitalists who are not as ruthlessly competitive will not survive, and the rise of unchecked monopolies will pervert the

Chains

CLASSICAL CONSERVATISM:

"We are all attached to the throne of the Supreme Being by a supple chain that restrains us without enslaving us."
—Joseph De Maistre, *Considerations on France* (1797)

CLASSICAL LIBERALISM:

"Man was born free, and everywhere he is in chains."
—Jean-Jacques Rousseau, *The Social Contract* (1762)

CLASSICAL SOCIALISM:

"The workers have nothing to lose in this but their chains. They have a world to gain. Workers of the world, unite!"
—Karl Marx, *The Communist Manifesto* (1848)

---

marketplace. Eventually the economy reaches the **crisis of capitalism**, a combination of three factors. First, there is massive *unemployment* owing to the capitalists' efforts to minimize numbers of employees and the inability of many enterprises to compete with the huge corporations. Second, there is an *overproduction* of goods—consumption cannot keep up with production. Specifically, the working class is paid so little that it cannot afford the goods being produced, so the economy begins to collapse. Third, the proletariat becomes *alienated* from their work and their role in society—they replace their civic sense (a false consciousness) with a class consciousness, that is, proletarian solidarity. Thus the crisis of capitalism will lead to revolution by the proletariat, just as the material changes in eighteenth-century feudal society led to the overthrow of the monarchies by the bourgeoisie.

Socialism

After proletarian revolution, the state would finally be in the hands of the majority. The workers, controlling the state, could now dictate policy. Marx believed the **dictatorship of the proletariat** would for the first time represent real democracy, because the means of production would finally be in the hands of the majority. The word *dictatorship* has been a source of conflict among Marxists; some argue that Marx simply meant rule by the working class, and others say it implies revolutionary decisiveness, a sort of temporary majoritarianism. During this time the bourgeoisie would become proletarians, losing their wealth as private property was abolished. Property would be expropriated from the owners and managed by the state. The peasantry would collectively work the land—for a salary, much like factory workers in the city; thus they would in effect become rural proletarians. Therefore, under **socialism** all classes would begin to merge into one. The hammer and sickle, symbol of communism, represents the unity of the proletariat and peasantry, and their eventual merger in a classless communist society.

In Marx's vision of a socialist economy, there would still be class distinctions and inequalities—for example, workers would be paid according to their worth, or contribution (incentive pay). But the crucial difference between socialism and capitalism is that in the socialist market there would be no private owner—therefore, no exploitation. In other words, the worker would receive true value in payment for labor.

Marx was initially skeptical of the likelihood of an evolutionary path to socialism, assuming that the bourgeoisie would not give up their wealth and power without violent revolution. However, near the end of his life he acknowledged the success that evolutionary socialist parties (and other reformist parties) were having, especially in European parliaments, and said that socialism might be achieved in increments, without revolution. Speaking in Amsterdam, he suggested it was especially likely in "America, England, and . . . perhaps . . . Holland."

Communism

Marx, like most intellectuals of his time, was fascinated with the pace of science and technology. Some today say he was naive to the limits to technological growth, because he saw virtually no end to the ability of science to "free" humanity from poverty and want. He believed that once a country had been industrialized through capital accumulation of the capitalist stage and finally fully developed (economically) in the most humanistic manner through socialism, communism could ultimately be reached.

Marx did not spell out a precise formula for **communism**. To do so, he said, would be to artificially prescribe a system that could hardly be imagined by those like himself who did not live in it and were thus ignorant of its nature. Those who live in a future communist society will freely determine its structure, he said. At any rate, Marx imagined a communist economy to be so completely developed for efficient, "scientifically planned" production—to meet human needs, not strictly for profit—that there would be material abundance and no poverty. All classes having completely merged into one, in effect, classes would no longer exist. Because he was convinced the state was nothing more than the tool of oppression for the dominant class (a means for justifying the exploitation of the lower classes), Marx saw no need for the continuation of the state as we know it, under communism. With no class to exploit, the state would become useless and "wither away." Coercive government would be replaced by "the administration of things," that is, by noncoercive bureaucracy. True democracy would finally be born. Of course, before a society could abolish its state, socialism would have to exist worldwide and the danger of war would have to have ended. By the time all societies had begun to complete socialist development, a new sense of internationalism would emerge and the whole world could finally reach communism together.

Because of the use of technology and machinery, the productivity of a scientifically planned future economy, the end to war and nationalism, the end to exploitation and wasteful capitalist competition, the end to the state and its ponderous bureaucracy, and so on, there would be such material abundance that money itself would no longer be necessary—people could simply take whatever they needed from public storehouses. In other words, they would be "paid" according to need rather than according to their contribution (as in socialism) or according to their market value (as in capitalism). A new communist individual (**the New Man**) would be born, free from all the social ills caused by exploitation, greed, envy, and inequality. Because of the end to private property, this new individual would have no reason to exploit others or covet their possessions and would internalize communalistic values, viewing his or her own prosperity as part of the whole society's progress. A collective spirit would prevail. At the same time, this person—freed of poverty and alienation—would be fully free to pursue his or her creative talents and interests in a truly individualistic manner. The individual would live to work and be creative, rather than work to live and pay bills.

MARX: SCIENTIST OR IDEOLOGUE?

It is easy to see how Marx's ideas could be very persuasive to poor workers as well as to upper-class intellectuals of his time. However, most people today believe Marx's vision—and especially his theory of communism—is a fantasy that can never be realized. Furthermore, the authoritarianism of so-called Marxist states like the former USSR and China has tarnished the image of Marxism.

Like all of us, Marx was to some degree a product of his time. His theory of communism reflects faith in science and technology and his vision of humanity conquering nature. Believing so strongly in rationalism and materialism, he thought that people would some day be capable of ridding the market of confusion, waste, and inefficiency by mastering the science of economic planning. Furthermore, his ideas of a future materially abundant society without marketplace constraints depends on an earth with no limits to material production and the exploitation of natural resources.

Marx's theory of economic determinism probably also overstates the importance of economics and neglects the role politics plays in determining economic structures. For example, the American labor movement's success at securing a higher standard of living for workers does not easily reconcile with Marx's view of the state and the class struggle. The occasional election of populist leaders who do battle with the wealthy elite of a country cannot be explained by Marx's belief in the state as a tool of the dominant class. Marx was born in 1818, and in his youth very few people in Western capitalist countries had voting rights. There was little chance that those with wealth and privilege would give up their power voluntarily, he thought. By the time of his death in 1883, the extension of democracy and voting rights was well under way, and only then did he recognize the possibility of democratic processes to bring about the changes he previously thought could be accomplished only through revolution. Similarly, his focus on economics tends to crowd out other important factors, such as culture, religion, and nationalism.

On the other hand, it is also clear that Marx was ahead of his time in many ways. Marx's ideas have swept the world, and many of his sociological concepts (especially the notion of alienation) are accepted even in capitalist countries today. Marx's analysis of a world in constant change contributed to the social scientific study of political evolution and economic development, rather than the traditional descriptive study of systems as they exist at the time. Most important, he focused the world's attention on the dynamic interplay between politics and economics more clearly than any philosopher, giving new and powerful substance to the field of *political economy*. It is probably fair to say that Marx's economic critique has made capitalism "kinder and gentler."

Modern socialists have redefined Marxism just as supporters of capitalism have redefined laissez-faire capitalism. And just as many versions of liberalism survive today, there are many variations and interpretations of Marxism as well. *Revisionist Marxists* have tried to reconcile Marxism with liberalism's pluralism and marketplace, creating hybrid models. *Humanist Marxists* study Marx's early writings on psychology, culture, and human alienation in modern industrial society. Those who focus on Marx's economics are generally called *orthodox Marxists*.

Those who claim to be communists today generally also claim to remain loyal to Marx's vision. When we refer to governments that are "communist," it is really a contradiction in terms—because in communism the state would have "withered away." It would be more appropriate to say "Communist-Party states," meaning that the country is governed by a Communist Party (that is, people claiming to believe in the eventual construction of communism). Note the distinction "claiming"—and remember, many people use ideological terms rhetorically or in order to cloak their real motivations. Just because some barbarous murderers such as Pol Pot's Khmer Rouge (the Cambodian "communists" who executed millions of their own people) claim to be communists or Marxists does not make them so. The same can be said of Saddam Hussein's claim to Arab nationalism—perhaps he has attempted to appear as a martyr to the Arab cause and more generally to Islam in order to mask his true power ambitions. And just because an authoritarian tyrant calls his political party the Democratic Party of Prosperity and Progress does not mean he is a democrat or that his policies promote prosperity or progress!

To repeat a point made earlier, even until the formal end of the Soviet Union, some people still called the Soviet system totalitarian. This reflects the legacy of Stalinism and confuses the discussion of the modern-day Soviet Union, which changed greatly since Stalin's death in 1953 and which began liberalizing (de-Stalinizing) long before the rise of Gorbachev. Many people also refer to communism when they really are talking about totalitarianism; Americans often say that the opposite of democracy is communism. Marx would roll over in his grave if he knew that people today associate a repressive, undemocratic government with communism.

MARXISM-LENINISM

Interpretations of Marxism abound: there is evolutionary socialism, Maoism, Titoism, Eurocommunism, Castroism, African socialism, and so on. But by far the most important interpretation was that of Lenin, the revolutionary leader of the Russian Revolution. Lenin was a Marxist, to be sure, but he added at least four important components to Marxism.

Imperialism

Socialists around the world were demoralized by the onset of World War I. Instead of achieving class unity and revolution against the bourgeoisie, the working class was fighting itself on the battlefields of Europe. Lenin explained that the coming of war rather than revolution was owing to imperialism. **Imperialism** refers to empire-building: the military acquisition of foreign colonies by an expansionist country. Imperialism is followed by colonialism: the administration or control over a dependent foreign territory, generally for the benefit of the imperial country. Writing in 1916, shortly before the Russian Revolution, Lenin described imperialism as the "final stage of capitalism." He said the capitalists had delayed the crisis of capitalism by expanding their markets overseas, selling products there and exploiting cheap labor and resources. Imperialism also promoted a sense of nationalism in the home country—which delayed proletarian class consciousness, as workers thought of themselves as conquering British (or French, etc.) rather than exploited proletarians, or the world working class. In fact, it even thrust them into the trenches to defend the imperial interests of their bourgeois capitalists—who were profiting from the war industry as well.

> "I have no country to fight for: my country is the earth, and I am a citizen of the world."
> —Eugene Debs (U.S. Socialist Party leader during World War I)

Lenin was not the first observer to describe the destructive effects of colonialism or to label it as imperialism. However, he was most responsible for spreading the theory of imperialism worldwide. These ideas were especially well received in the decolonizing countries of South Asia and Africa, where many revolutionaries—both communist and noncommunist—adapted Lenin's theories to their own colonial situation.

Mao Zedong, the Chinese Communist leader, was especially influenced by Lenin's description of imperialist exploitation, because it seemed to explain so well what had been done to China by foreign powers. Lenin, Mao, and other revolutionaries in less-developed countries considered their countries to be the "weak link" in the chain of international capitalism. So, although imperialism breathed new life into capitalism in the industrially-developed world, it also brought the rest of the world into the coming international socialist revolution. Whereas Marx studied the class struggle on the level of individual countries, Lenin argued that the international class struggle was just as important, because capitalism had internationalized. This was a departure from Marx, who predicted socialist revolution in developed capitalist societies, not in peasant-based feudalistic societies.

The Necessity of Revolution

Lenin feared evolutionary socialism, which he derisively referred to as "economism" and "opportunism." He observed the incremental successes that socialist parties, such as the German Social Democratic Party (SPD), were achieving. To him, they were trivial and served to quiet the proletariat, preventing revolutionary class consciousness and real change. Lenin was not interested in reform, because it would only interfere with more fundamental progress. He advised communists to *agitate* (campaign) and *propagandize* (spread ideas and arguments) for revolution only.

The Party

The success of the revolution would depend on political organization. Lenin's political party was designed to help create the revolution, not just to be there when that "inevitable" moment came. Lenin was not terribly optimistic of the ability of the working class to lead themselves in socialist revolution. No doubt he was accurate in his perception of the average person's understanding of politics. This elitist attitude (plus the fact that most of the Russian people were still illiterate peasants at the time) made him advocate a small **vanguard party** of "professional revolutionaries"—disciplined ideologues—rather than a large party, such as the German SPDs. Further, Lenin's party (the Bolshevik Party) was at first illegal in Russia, so it had to be small and disciplined. Decisions were to be made on the principle of what Lenin called **democratic centralism**—meaning that debate on policy was free and open, but that members were expected to obey decisions once they were voted on and passed.

"Democracy for an insignificant minority, democracy for the rich—that is the democracy of capitalist society. If we look more closely into the machinery of capitalist democracy, we shall see everywhere, in the 'petty'—supposedly petty—details of the suffrage [author's note: right to vote] (residential qualification, exclusion of women, etc.), in the technique of the representative assembly (public buildings are not for 'beggars'!), in the purely capitalist organization of the daily press, etc., etc.— we shall see restriction after restriction upon democracy. These restrictions, exceptions, exclusions, obstacles for the poor, seem slight, especially in the eyes of one who has never known want himself and has never been in close contact with the oppressed classes in their mass life . . . but in their sum total these restrictions exclude and squeeze out the poor from politics, from active participation in democracy.

   Marx grasped this essence of capitalist democracy splendidly, when . . . he said that the oppressed are allowed once every few years to decide which particular representatives of the oppressing class shall represent and repress them in parliament!"
   —Vladimir Lenin, The State and Revolution, Chapter 5, part 2
                                                         (August 1917)

That Lenin thought of himself as democratic might sound absurd to those who are aware of his disdain for Western "bourgeois democratic parliaments." Liberals generally define democracy procedurally; that is, the process of free elections, political debate, legislative representation, and the like is what they call democracy. Lenin thought this to be a sham and argued that it did little to improve the lives of the masses. **Procedural democracy** can be contrasted with **substantive democracy**. Lenin argued that a political system is democratic to the degree that it directly acts in the best interests of the majority, which is what he believed his party was doing.

Critics of Lenin, including Russians, have often made the point that Lenin's strict party organization led to authoritarian government practices in the Soviet Union. That is, the revolutionary means were retained even after the seizure of power, in effect creating a nondemocratic government structure that allowed no criticism and expected obedient conformism. Defenders of Lenin answer that he was forced to use authoritarian tactics out of military necessity during the Russian civil war, as are all leaders in wartime. They blame Soviet authoritarianism on Stalin instead. Since Lenin died so soon after the revolution and civil war (in 1924), the question of whether Lenin begat Stalin remains a contentious debate.

Of course, Lenin believed in Marx's notion of the *New Man*—that individuals freed of poverty and exploitation would be cooperative and just. In this view, internally individuals are good; if only they are liberated from the enslavement of the class struggle, their true being will emerge. The American Founding Fathers, on the other hand, believed that individuals were fundamentally selfish and competitive and that these natural traits necessitated separation of power, coupled with checks and balances. Lenin's confidence in the character of his "vanguard" party members, combined with the need for secrecy before the revolution and the immediacy of fighting the civil war after the revolution, resulted in a nearly total neglect of checks and balances. In his final days, Lenin began to worry about Stalin's potential rise to power and wrote a warning to his fellow party members about Stalin. Few took him seriously, because Stalin was considered a relatively unsophisticated and unimportant member of the party leadership at the time. However, Stalin's willingness to be ruthless, coupled with the absence of checks against the Soviet Communist Party leadership, eventually allowed him to seize complete control of the country.

State Capitalism

In 1917, Russia was hardly a developed capitalist country—which, according to Marx, was the precondition for socialism. Many Marxists (at

The Many Meanings of the Term Communism

What exactly does the term *communism* mean? Unfortunately for the student of ideology, the answer will depend on the circumstances and person using the word. The original utopian usage of the word referred mainly to a communalistic sharing of resources, duties, and benefits. Marx's and Engel's communism referred to a futuristic planned society of material abundance and social harmony. Lenin's (and later, China's and others') Communist Party made communism a revolutionary political movement advocating Marxism and equated the Soviet Union with communism. Stalin's rule of the Soviet Union condemned communism to mean totalitarianism. The de-Stalinization of the Soviet Union under Khrushchev and later Soviet leaders left the term to mean what was then a more accurate description of the Soviet Union: authoritarian socialism (an authoritarian political system with a socialist economy). Lenin's and Mao's writings on imperialism associated communism with the colonial world's independence struggle against the Western imperial countries. Among Eurocommunists (Western European communists) it can mean anything from classical Marxism to Soviet-style socialism to democratic socialism. In poor countries of the developing world the term is often used by the ruling party purely because of its populist propaganda value, since their impoverished citizens may be more inclined to trust such a political party than one that more explicitly appeals to the business elite of the country. Therefore, in practice, *communism* may mean:

- a communal utopia (such as More's utopianism)
- an advanced economic form (as per Marx's vision)
- a revolutionary political movement (Lenin's party)
- the Soviet Union (the first Communist Party-led state)
- totalitarianism (Stalinism)
- authoritarian socialism (as practiced by several countries)
- anti-imperialism (because of Lenin's and others' writings)
- Eurocommunism (Western European communism)
- a populist party (in the developing world)

In summary, communism, like many ideological terms (e.g., democracy), means different things to different people. This, and these terms' frequent deliberate misuse for rhetorical purposes, considerably confuse ideological discourse. The many meanings of *communism* also illustrate how important it is that people use a common vocabulary when debating ideology—or, failing that, at least that they understand each others' use of the terms.

first even the majority of his Bolshevik Party members) argued with Lenin over the feasibility of revolution, ahead of Marx's schedule, so to speak. In Marxian terms, the Russian empire was still basically a feudal society: capitalism and the proletarian class were only now developing. Lenin's important change was the notion that socialist revolutions could "skip the capitalist stage" and economically develop the country through the leadership of the Communist Party rather than through capitalist investors. After the civil war ended, Lenin's solution was to allow limited capitalism in the country, under the guidance of state regulation (the New Economic Policy [NEP]), until the economy could be developed enough to create socialism. No one knows just how long he expected this to last, because when Lenin died in 1924 Stalin took over and reversed course, claiming the NEP had accomplished its goals. Many developing countries today claim to use **state capitalism** as a compromise between capitalism and socialism. In some ways it may remind the reader of corporatism, although its goal is different.

Leninism after the Breakup of the Soviet Union

Until shortly before the demise of the Soviet Union, almost all Soviet officials loosely evoked **Leninism** to identify practically anything good and proper. Lenin's name was used by anyone who advocated anything, in an attempt to show that Lenin had spoken in favor of the idea—or at least that he would have endorsed it. Everyone from Stalin to Gorbachev claimed to be a *Leninist*, as if that gave them some particular insight in how to produce energy, explore space, oversee medicine, build day-care centers, and negotiate arms control agreements. In reality, Lenin was a revolutionary ideologue—he had little time to think of (or write about) how to run a country. Now that the ideological taboos of Soviet and Russian politics have been broken, even Leninism has been repudiated by most, although Lenin remains a heroic figure to many Russians and to some nationalists in the less-developed world. Even some who blame him for allowing the rise of Stalinism credit him for ending the reign of the tsars. Lenin will probably remain a hero to those in the newly formed republics who blame the disintegration of the Soviet Union and the end of the Communist Party for the terrible economic condition their country is in as it undergoes the painful transition to a mixed economy.

DEMOCRATIC SOCIALISM

Marxism probably had its greatest effect on Eastern Europe where it blended with one-party authoritarianism and even totalitarianism under

---

Figure 8-1

pluralism

democratic capitalism	**democratic socialism**
(classical liberalism or liberal capitalism)	(similar to evolutionary socialism)

capitalism ———————————————— **socialism**

authoritarian capitalism	**authoritarian socialism**
(sometimes [erroneously] called "fascism")	(often called "communism")

authoritarianism

Stalin. It has even meshed with nationalism *(a strange partnership!)* in revolutionary movements in the developing world. Western European socialist ideology, however, is a mixture of liberalism, Marxism, and non-Marxist socialism that is generally called **democratic socialism**. Western European political parties that adhere to principles of democratic socialism are today partners in government with liberal parties. They accept the legitimate role of the state and a pluralistic political system. Although they downplay the importance of the class struggle, they do advocate redistribution of wealth and opportunity.

Marx has no monopoly on socialist thought. As mentioned previously, utopian socialists preceded Marx. After Marx's works became well known, a number of *revisionist* movements arose to challenge some of his ideas, including the British Fabians, the social democrats (whose ideas emerged in Germany but quickly spread throughout Europe), and later the Eurocommunists (particularly in Italy and France).

Democratic socialists believe that socialism is the economic extension of democracy. They argue that the great disparity in wealth that is inherent in free enterprise capitalism is undemocratic and politically corrupting. If not restrained, wealthy individuals can use their economic power to manipulate elections, the press, political parties, interest groups, and politicians for their own benefit. In such cases, pluralism is a fraud. The super-rich largely control the social agenda, the educational establishment, the workplace, and even the development of culture, making social equality and individualism scarce. They can also monopolize trade, deceive consumers, and make private profits at great costs to society, subverting the merits of supply and demand. Their appetite for personal property can leave the bulk of the citizenry indebted renters, making a mockery of the liberal promise of private property. Democratic socialists believe that only through socialism are the worthy liberal ideals of individualism, equality, pluralism, liberty, and even property *truly* achievable.

Key Terms

commune
social Darwinists
Marxism
utopians
dialectics
materialism
class struggle
economic determinism
proletariat
surplus value
false consciousness
alienation
crisis of capitalism

dictatorship of the proletariat
socialism
communism
the New Man
imperialism
vanguard party
democratic centralism
procedural democracy
substantive democracy
state capitalism
Leninism
democratic socialism

Study Questions

1. What were some of the early socialist criticisms of laissez-faire capitalism, and in what historical context did it emerge?
2. What did Marx mean by utopian socialism?
3. What is dialectics, and how did Marx apply the concept to the class struggle?
4. What is economic determinism, and what was Marx's theory of social progress through historical eras?
5. What is the difference between socialism and communism, in Marx's terms?
6. What is the difference between Marx's vision of communism and most Americans' conception of what communism means?
7. What elements of Marxism have endured and shaped our society today? What are some of Marxism's most obvious flaws?
8. What is the impact and legacy of Lenin on Marxism?
9. How does Western European socialism differ from the Stalinist application of Marxism?

10. In light of the rise of Stalin, what argument would Locke, Montesquieu, and the American Founding Fathers make if they could speak with Lenin?

CHAPTER 9

FASCISM

THE RISE OF FASCISM

During the seventeenth and eighteenth centuries the two largest ideological forces in the world were classical conservatism and classical liberalism. Although they were opposing sides of the great ideological battle over the reform of feudal monarchism, they also shared some common ground. By the middle of the nineteenth century it was clear that liberalism had emerged victorious, although conservatism had made its impact, and the struggle against authoritarianism continues in new forms. However, classical liberalism was immediately challenged by another great movement—classical socialism.

Since the mid-nineteenth century, liberalism and socialism have dominated world ideological thought. It is commonly thought that they too offer radically different visions of the way the world should be. Their greatest differences lie in the area of economics. However, in many ways they are more similar than liberalism and conservatism were. Both liberalism and socialism are guided by the rationalism of the Enlightenment. Both assume the fundamental equality of all human beings and offer salvation to all. Both promote progressive change toward a bright future for humanity. Both promise economic systems capable of delivering abundant material wealth. Both envision a constant human process of harnessing, controlling, and ultimately defeating the forces of the natural world, in the name of human freedom and progress. However, the twentieth century witnessed the emergence of a new ideological movement—**fascism**—that confronted both liberalism and socialism.

> "I go the way that Providence dictates with the assurance of a sleepwalker."
>
> —Adolf Hitler

Fascism is to a large degree a historically defined ideology. It was created by historical experience—specifically that of fascist Italy and Nazi Germany preceding and during World War II. Various liberal and Marxist revolutions were led by ideologues who had studied philosophy and tried to apply it. Conversely, fascism was a revolution in search of an ideology. In other words, the leaders of Italian and German fascism, Benito Mussolini and Adolf Hitler, did not have a rich ideological base to guide them in their efforts. They created most of it themselves, through practice rather than theory.

In Europe, the period following World War I was marked by an unusual instability in governments, social turmoil, and great hardships—including eventually a worldwide economic depression. Germany suffered from both hyperinflation and unemployment. Many veterans of the war, including Hitler himself, were embittered by defeat and claimed they had been betrayed by treasonous politicians who ended the war too soon, when Germany still could have won. In such an atmosphere, appeals to nationalism enjoyed attentive audiences. Similarly, certain Italian politicians complained that even though Italy, as an Allied power, had helped defeat the Central Powers, it was being left out of the postwar negotiations. Some Italians felt they were not being treated as a full and equal ally of the victorious French, British, and Americans. Italy was also racked with economic hardship and was particularly immobilized by frequent labor strikes.

Those societies that had suffered the most from the destruction and stress of the war, such as Germany and Russia, were the most prone to consider radical solutions to their problems. In 1917, Lenin's Bolshevik Party came to power in the collapsing Russian empire. Many Europeans feared the spread of communism to their countries. Probably nowhere was this anti-communist sentiment greater than in Germany and Italy, where well-organized Marxist parties were active.

Mussolini came to prominence in Italy as the leader of a radical group of World War I veterans who created vigilante-style *squadre* ("squads") of *fasci di combattimento* ("combat groups") that made use of intimidation, beatings, and even murder to disrupt labor strikes, peasant land squatters, Marxist party activities, and left-wing newspapers. Mussolini's *squadre* were often supported financially and otherwise by wealthy industrialists and landowners. They wore black shirts (thus the name **blackshirts**) to mimic the uniforms of the World War I Italian *arditi* ("shock troops"). Hitler organized similar gangs (the Stormtroopers, also mimicking World War I–era elite troops), who wore distinctive brown shirts. The **brown-shirts** violently attacked German socialists and communists and eventually tried unsuccessfully to overthrow the government. In prison for the attempt, Hitler wrote *Mein Kampf* (My Struggle) in which he explained his ideology and goals. In both cases, these armed organizations became the heart of the growing fascist movements.

In 1922 Mussolini was appointed prime minister of Italy, partially by convincing the king that he was needed to restore order and partially by threatening to seize power if he was ignored. In 1933 the German president appointed Hitler chancellor for much the same reasons. Although conservatives and liberals alike in both countries feared Mussolini and Hitler, most were even more concerned about the communists and were furthermore moved by the fascist appeals to nationalism.

NATIONALISM

As mentioned in Chapter 3, fascism is in part an extreme form of nationalism. Adolf Hitler's Nazi ("not-see") Party preached an extreme form of fascism, what is today known as **Nazism** (Naziism). The term *Nazi* comes from the abbreviated party title "National Socialists," which had nothing to do with socialism and everything to do with nationalism. (Hitler used the term *socialist* primarily for its propaganda value—it was an almost universally positive term in Europe at that time.) Hitler used nationalism to rebuild the shattered German economy and military during the interwar period (between World War I and World War II). He did this in large part by uniting Germany through patriotic symbolism and mythology. Mussolini did the same in Italy. Each form of fascist nationalism exploded into militarism, expansionist aggression, and extremely reactionary social policies.

> "I offer neither pay, nor quarters, nor provisions; I offer hunger, thirst, forced marches, battles, and death. Let him who loves his country in his heart and not with his lips only, follow me."
> —Giuseppe Garibaldi

Germany and Italy were especially subject to nationalist manipulation. Neither had become fully unified into modern nation-states until the early 1870s, so both were highly conscious of their national identity. Italy was home to one of the best-known nationalist thinkers, Giuseppe Mazzini, who along with Giuseppe Garibaldi and Victor Emmanuel II led the unification effort. Each of these men were dead by the end of World War I, and Mussolini largely filled the void. Mazzini's nationalism rejected many aspects of liberalism, especially individualism. He was more interested in freedom for nations than liberty for individuals. He felt that any individualistic behavior or ideas that stood in the way of national unity and independence should be repressed. Ideas like these would later be incorporated into Mussolini's nationalism.

Hitler's nation—"the Aryan people"—were not specifically the German people; German Jews were not Aryans, and still others were considered Aryan even though they were citizens of foreign countries. **Aryan** is a term used by linguists to name an ancient warrior tribe that is thought to have invaded what is now India and Iran from Europe and northern Asia approximately 3,500 years ago. Linguists have identified numerous similarities between European and southern Asian languages, and so have theorized they must have a common lingual root in the Aryan people, who spoke an Indo-European language. Various Europeans later theorized that the blond-haired, blue-eyed Aryans from northern Europe must have been a highly advanced and powerful civilization to force their language on so many people across southern Europe and Asia. They must have been the ruling class of such societies, which explains much of their ancient technology and wisdom, according to these theorists. However, as the Aryans mixed with "inferior," darker-skinned people, the Aryan stock became diluted, resulting in less-talented people. For Hitler, the solution was clear—the Aryan nation, a "master race," must be kept pure and unpolluted by inferior peoples. This racial elite could include other Aryans from northern Europe, especially "Nordics" from Scandinavia, but no others. To aid in racial purification, the Nazis created a program of **eugenics** (a selective breeding plan to improve the national gene pool, by breeding intelligent, blond-haired, blue-eyed German men and women, and by weeding out undesirable, non-Aryan characteristics).

ELITISM

The two best proofs of the extreme elitism of Nazism were the death camps and the eugenics program. Hitler's racist nationalism generated the wholesale scapegoating of Jews, Slavs, and darker-skinned people for virtually all of Germany's problems. Jews, as a minority in a Christian culture, had long been subject to suspicion, prejudice, and mistreatment (**anti-Semitism**) in Europe. Anti-Semitism is rooted in the belief that Jews were responsible for the crucifixion of Christ; it involved the retaliatory restriction of European Jews to certain unpopular professions. However, under liberalism they fared better and were slowly winning social and political equality. Many conservatives blamed social problems on the increasing acceptance of Jews in public life. Hitler was particularly obsessed with the danger posed to Aryans by Jews, whom he called the "destroyers" of Aryan culture. According to him, Jews, although inferior, were dangerously clever and were engaged in a worldwide conspiracy to take over institutions of business and government and eventually enslave the Aryans. Once in power, Hitler steadily increased the persecution of Jews and other minorities, eventually reaching the "final solution"—the attempted genocide of all European Jews. **Genocide** refers to the systematic attempt to exterminate a race, nation, or ethnic group through government-organized mass murder. Approximately six million Jews were killed by the Nazis, mostly during the last years of World War II, in a period today called **the Holocaust**. Also included in the Holocaust were communists, Slavs, Gypsies, homosexuals, the disabled, those with terminal diseases or mental illnesses, children born with deformities, unwitting victims of medical experimentation, and political enemies. Their murders were justified in the name of building the Aryan master race.

Fascist Italy was originally only marginally more anti-Semitic than other European countries. However, under the influence of Hitler, Mussolini grew increasingly anti-Semitic as well. The Italian fascists did not practice *systematic* genocide; but in Italian-occupied Ethiopia, Mussolini's troops frequently committed massacres of the native population and attacked any large concentrations of Ethiopian resistance fighters with poison gas.

Less well known is fascism's anti-feminism. Fascists considered both liberal and socialist attempts to promote social equality to be unnatural and impossible in practice. Elitism fit well with their theories on race and their glorification of the virtuous male soldier. Even blond-haired, blue-eyed Aryan women were treated as second-class citizens by the fascists. Among Aryan men there were also rare and superior individuals, more fit to lead. This natural elite was called the **ubermensch** (literally, "overman"; i.e., superman), a term coined by the German philosopher Nietzsche, who influenced Hitler in a variety of ways. Every leader of the Nazi Party was considered to be an *ubermensch*.

MILITARISM

Fascists glorified war and the martial spirit. To fascists, the organization and command of the military is perhaps more important than even the control of the ruling political party. Both Mussolini and Hitler were heavily influenced by their experiences as low-ranking soldiers in World War I. As political leaders, both enjoyed wearing military uniforms and giving orders to their generals. Consider the fascist slogans in the accompanying text box, each probably coined by Mussolini.

> "Blood alone moves the wheels of history."
> "Nothing has ever been won without bloodshed."
> "War is to a man what motherhood is to a woman."
> "Believe, obey, fight."
> —Italian fascist slogans

The fascists' martial spirit, combined with nationalism and racism, led naturally to an aggressive, expansionist foreign policy. Fascist foreign policy was further justified by social Darwinism (discussed in Chapter 8). Hitler and Mussolini both believed that war was natural and necessary for human progress—that it cleansed the world of the weak and inferior nations, just as natural selection eliminates members of the species that are relatively weak. This militarist foreign policy is sometimes referred to as **international social Darwinism**. Fascists argue that peace is an unnatural state that cannot last long, which is good because conflict builds a strong citizenry that is willing to die for their nation. War, and thereby sacrifice to the nation, is the best test of an individual's worth.

ORGANICISM

Like the classical conservatives, fascists rejected individualism as an obstacle to the whole organism. However, the organism of concern to fascists was the nation-state, that is, the Italian people and the Aryan people and their governments. Fascists believe that individuals are only meaningful as parts of the nation and should give up their individuality to the state that represents the nation.

Similarly, they rejected the *anti-statism* of the liberals and Marxists. To liberals, the state was a necessary evil that had to be continually checked and restrained to prevent its intrusion into the economy, religion, and the affairs of individuals. To Marxists, the state was a tool of oppression for the dominant class, used to exploit the lower classes. Fascists, on the other hand, were **statists** and glorified the state as the ultimate expression of the nation.

The organicism of the fascists is further illustrated by their economic ideology, *corporatism* or *corporativism*, which was also neither liberal nor socialist. However, the corporatist economic ideology outlined in Chapter 5 differs substantially from fascist economics. Political scientists call it **societal corporatism** to distinguish it from fascist **state corporatism**. The difference lies in whether the various corporate units are formed through economic incentives and freely cooperate for their own benefit (as in societal corporatism), or whether the corporate units are created by and are subservient to the interests of the state (as in state corporatism). Furthermore, in the case of Italian state corporatism, it formed the basis of *political* pseudo-representation as well. By 1934 Mussolini had organized the Italian economy into twenty-two corporations, each of which elected representatives to the Chamber of Fasces and Corporations, which by 1938 replaced the powerless Italian parliament. However, critics of both Italian and German fascist economics argue that corporatism was merely a cover for the ruthless economic exploitation of the working class. For example, only industrial and business elites were truly represented in Italy's corporatist governing structure, because representatives of labor tended to be Mussolini's puppets.

This does not mean that there is a necessary link between corporatism and fascism; most governments take at least partial control of their economies (especially in planning the arms industries) in time of war, as the United States did during World War II.

ANTI-INTELLECTUALISM

The fascists also rejected rationalism. Their philosophy in this regard has much in common with the classical conservatives' irrationalism. To repeat, irrationalists argue that human society and nature are infinitely complex and beyond the scope of human understanding. Therefore, society must be guided by decisions based on elements other than reason and the scientific process. For fascists, instinct, will, and emotion are higher forms of understanding than reason.

> "Think with your blood!"
>
> —Benito Mussolini

The fascist philosophy is probably more appropriately labeled **anti-intellectualism**, because it was rooted more in ignorance of philosophy than in the intellectual position of the irrationalists. One has only to consider the frequent Nazi book-burnings to appreciate the anti-intellectual nature of its ideology. Mussolini and Hitler ridiculed abstract philosophy and reasoning, arguing that people are motivated by passion, emotion, instinct, mysticism, superstition, fears, experience, and prejudices—not by ideas and logic. In their view, if the masses are given appropriate motivators, a powerful national force will result. Action, not thought, is what matters in politics. This makes practical strategy and tactics more important than utopian ideals studied by social scientists who never act upon their theories. For this reason, fascists obsessively constructed symbols, propaganda, slogans, and myths and used education, culture, religion, art, and music to spread them. Whereas philosophy moves elites, the masses would be mobilized behind fascism primarily through nationalist symbolism and mythmongering. Probably the most important symbols were the fasces and the swastika, the symbols of Italian fascism and German Nazism and the centerpieces of their national flags during the fascist era.

> "The broad mass of a nation . . . will more easily fall victim to a big lie than to a small one."
>
> —Adolf Hitler

The term *fascism* is derived from the word *fasces*. A **fasces** is a bundle of rods or sticks, which—tied together with an ax-like blade—represented ancient Roman authority, unity, and justice. Italian fascists compared the strength of the fasces with the potential strength of the united Italian people. The fasces served as an excellent symbol, because it simultaneously symbolized modern Italian nationalism and reminded Italians of the greatness and power of the Roman Empire. It also complemented the fascists' advocacy of organicism and corporatism, because it stood for national unity. Prior to World War II, many countries used the fasces symbol in various ways, although it has now been somewhat tarnished. It does remain, however, on the back of U.S. dimes and on each side of the flag that hangs behind the chair of the Speaker of the House in the U.S. House of Representatives.

The term **swastika** is derived from the Sanskrit (a primarily Indian language) *svastika*, which means "welfare" or "good luck." The swastika is thought to be at least 5,000 years old and has been found (in various forms) in ancient cultures around the world (including China, Polynesia, southern Europe, the Americas, and the Middle East), which is not surprising given its simplicity in form. It has symbolized the sun, the cycle of life and death, and the concept of infinity and eternity—all powerful concepts. Upon learning of its discovery in both Scandinavia and India, Hitler decided it must be an Aryan symbol, spread throughout the world with the Aryan (Indo-European) language, and adopted it as his Nazi symbol, although he reversed it and tilted it 45 degrees. Today the term *swastika* refers not only to the Asian *svastika* but also to the Byzantine and Greek *gammadion cross* and the Nazi *Hakenkreuz* ("hooked cross").

AUTHORITARIANISM

As discussed in Chapter 4, Nazi Germany was a totalitarian state. Mussolini declared Italy to be totalitarian as well. Obviously, Italian fascism was extremely authoritarian; however, Mussolini never completely controlled Italy in the way that Hitler controlled Germany. The biggest obstacle to Mussolini's totalitarian goal was the Catholic Church (specifically the Vatican, located within Rome itself), with which he had an ambiguous relationship.

"Mussolini is always right."

—Italian fascist slogan

What Italian fascism and German fascism did have in common was autocratism. Their entire fascist regimes were built around single leaders, *Der Führer* and *il Duce* ("the leader," in German and Italian, respectively). Hitler and Mussolini defined fascism. Both were idolized as unique historical figures of iron will and ingenious leadership. Each encouraged a **cult of personality**, or hero worship of a charismatic figure. This was an especially important feature of propaganda, given the anti-intellectual nature of fascist ideology. It gave the people something concrete and real in which to believe.

Hitler saw himself as a savior whose destiny it was to awaken the dormant Aryan nation. In his view, although the Aryans were an advanced and civilized nation they were being deceived by Jewish cunning (an argument not unlike the cold war fear of the superior American system being subverted by an inferior but diabolical communist conspiracy). Therefore, the autocratism of a bold, willful, instinctively creative *ubermensch* was necessary to lead the nation through the struggle for greatness and rebuild the master race.

When Mussolini and Hitler both died in 1945, the fascist movement and its blind faith largely disintegrated, even in other countries. There have been other semi-fascists, such as Franco of Spain and Perón of Argentina, whose deaths also resulted in the decomposition of their political movements. This is typical of other autocratic systems as well, because so much of the movement is based on a cult of personality rather than on a well-defined ideology.

MODERN FASCISM

Until 1994 the clearest example of modern-day fascism was the apartheid regime of South Africa. **Apartheid** (meaning "apart-hood") was the former South African government policy of segregating its citizens into white, colored (mixed), Asian, and black. It also referred to the massive political, economic, and social discrimination against nonwhites, and especially against the black majority. However, reform led by former president F. W. de Klerk has finally dismantled apartheid and instituted majority rule. The African National Congress leader Nelson Mandela, who was imprisoned by the former South African government, is now South Africa's president. Most white South Africans support majority (black) rule and the end of apartheid. Nonetheless, there remains a violent minority of embittered whites who consider the reform a betrayal. Fascist groups such as the Afrikaner Resistance Movement (ARM) have threatened the government.

With the end of apartheid, some may be tempted to say fascism is finally dead. There is always the danger of complacency regarding its reemergence. For the last few decades a few pseudo-historians have tried to revise history, claiming there was no Holocaust—no death camps, no gas chambers, and no "final solution." Remembering World War II and the Holocaust, much of the world has continually repeated the pledge *"never again."* Yet when systematic mass murder and aggression occurs today (in Bosnia, Rwanda and Burundi, Sri Lanka, or elsewhere) the world community is slow to act, if it is willing at all. There are now a wide variety of active fascist movements around the world. Fascist political parties have sprung up all over Europe, such as the British National Party, the Russian Liberal Democratic Party, the French National Front, and many others. Even in modern Germany, economic difficulties in the region of the former East Germany coupled with large numbers of foreign immigrants has added fuel to the fire of a growing neo-Nazi movement. In Italy, Mussolini's granddaughter, Alessandra Mussolini, is now a member of parliament, representing the growing fascist National Alliance Party.

The very real danger of a fascist coming to power in the instability that now exists in Russia is especially frightening. Extremist candidates

Deja Vu?

	GERMANY, 1930s	RUSSIA, 1990s
misleading party name:	National Socialist Party	Liberal Democratic Party
economic situation in country:	depression, hyperinflation	depression, hyperinflation
government stability:	attempted coups	attempted coups
domestic tranquility:	brownshirt violence	Mafia violence
recent territorial changes:	World War I losses	disintegration of USSR
nationalistic resentment:	of World War I victors	of "cold war victors"
scapegoats:	non-Aryans, especially Jews	non-Russian former Soviets
greatest political enemies:	Liberals, Communists	Liberals, Communists
promises to military:	restore the German military	restore the Soviet military
Western view of fascist leader:	"tramp," "madman"	"fool," "clown"

generally have a better chance getting elected in difficult times. The most obviously fascist Russian party, the ironically labeled Liberal Democratic Party (LDP), under the leadership of a demagogue named Vladimir Zhirinovsky, won about 25 percent in the 1993 Russian parliamentary elections. Although the LDP received only 11 percent in the 1995 parliamentary elections (because of the large number of parties) this amounted to a second-place finish, behind the Communists and ahead of Boris Yeltsin's supporters. Only one other party cleared the minimum 5 percent threshold required to win parliamentary seats. In 1996, Zhirinovsky captured only 6 percent of the vote in the presidential election, losing ground to the Communist Party candidate Gennadi Zyuganov, who campaigned as a supernationalist as well. Many voters indicated they would vote for whichever of the two had the best chance of defeating Yeltsin. (Yeltsin won the run-off against Zyuganov, in part owing to help from American campaign advisors.)   At any rate, there are striking parallels between the circumstances in Germany that gave rise to Hitler and the current state of affairs in Russia.

In the United States there is an assortment of white supremacists, violent skinheads, and organizations such as the Ku Klux Klan, Aryan Nations, and The Order, each of which embrace fascism and Nazism. Most Americans dismiss these isolated neo-fascists as powerless in American politics and society. However, even among the better-organized, self-proclaimed superpatriots in the survivalist or militia movements, who often claim to reject fascism, there are disturbing similarities: virulent nationalism, militarism, racism, anti-intellectualism, symbol worship, and authoritarian tendencies. However, their near hatred of the state puts them closer to the ideology of anarchists than fascists in this respect.

Ethnocentrism or Ethnosupremacy?

Outright fascists are generally easy to spot. In some cases, however, intolerance and anti-intellectualism sometimes come in smaller doses; there is a fine line between pride in one's heritage and bigotry. **Ethnocentrists** glorify the role and importance of their own ethnic or national group. They place it at the *center* of history, culture, science, ideological thought, and so on. Is this healthy self-esteem or racial supremacy?

Since the bombing of the federal building in Oklahoma City, the press has brought the ideas of various militia movements to the public's attention. Many militia members, survivalists, and tax resisters accuse the U.S. government of a massive plot to deprive white Christian Americans of their natural rights. These ethnocentrists often claim that they are not themselves racist but simply want to protect their constitutional rights from a left-wing government "taken over by Jews, blacks, and illegal immigrants." They concoct bizarre conspiracy theories about the United Nations, Chinese communists, and international banks.

Ethnocentrism can be found in all ethnic communities. *Afrocentrism* originally referred to the broad academic movement whose goal is the promotion of the study of African culture, history, science, and so on— something that most Americans now realize has been largely neglected in public education. However, it has recently spawned a few radical Afrocentrists who have popularized incredible myths about evil white (often Jewish) scientists creating AIDS and other diseases to kill African Americans. They have also claimed that white politicians (in "AmeriKKKa") have purposely encouraged the illegal sales of narcotics and handguns in African-American neighborhoods in order to commit "genocide" against African Americans. Some ethnocentrists ("melanists") even claim that darker-skinned people have a superior understanding of truth because they learn instinctively and emotionally rather than through the "flawed" European-dominated scientific process. Such rhetoric is hauntingly similar to the anti-intellectualism of Hitler and Mussolini.

Although such sentiments may not be as dangerous as is the ideology of the armed militias (and although neither can be reasonably called fascism), both act to divide Americans and promote suspicion and resentment. Ethnocentric mythmongers, be they white or black, leftists or rightists, Americans or Bosnian Serbs, sow the seeds of fascism.

> "I am waiting in the wings. My moment has nearly arrived."
> —Vladimir Zhirinovsky

Although the rise to power of fascists is at present unlikely in any country, it could occur anywhere there is resentment, unemployment, social turmoil and disorder, and willing ears for a charismatic speaker. World War II provides ample evidence that the rise of fascism in any single country presents a danger to all others.

Key Terms

fascism
blackshirts, brownshirts
Nazism
Aryan
eugenics
anti-Semitism
genocide
the Holocaust
ubermensch
international social Darwinism

statism
societal corporatism
state corporatism
anti-intellectualism
fasces
swastika
cult of personality
apartheid
ethnocentrism

Study Questions

1. In what ways are classical liberalism and classical socialism similar, as compared to fascism? In what ways are fascists similar to the classical conservatives?
2. What is meant by the phrases "fascism is to a large degree a historically defined ideology" and "fascism was a revolution in search of an ideology"?
3. In what circumstances did Italian and German fascism emerge, and in what circumstances might it be reborn today?
4. What were the components of Italian and German fascism? Explain how each concept contributed to fascism.
5. What are the most important symbols of fascism? What are the origins of these symbols?
6. Does fascism survive as a modern ideological movement? Who are the fascists of today?

CHAPTER 10

ENVIRONMENTALISM

WHAT IS ENVIRONMENTALISM?

The environment is generally defined as the world of conditions and things that surrounds something else, such as us humans. However, it has a particular ideological meaning that can be more accurately labeled the **biosphere** or **ecosphere**. That is, common usage of the term *environment* is generally synonymous with the terms *biosphere* and *ecosphere*. Specifically, the biosphere is the area of the earth within which life is sustained, such as the outer crust of the earth, the sea, and the troposphere (the lower part of the atmosphere). Within the biosphere, ecological systems, or **ecosystems**, exist. An ecosystem is an interdependent complex of organisms, including both plants and animals, that sustain each other's life and reproduction. The global community of ecosystems and their biosphere make up the ecosphere.

Who is an **environmentalist**? An environmentalist is one who wants to protect the ecosphere from the ongoing assault of human activity that is resulting in pollution, ecological destruction, resource depletion, and overpopulation. Loosely defined as such, this could include almost everyone. However, environmentalists as ideologues might be better defined as those whose *primary* ideological value and motivation is the protection of the ecosphere.

IDEOLOGY OR ISSUE?

Is environmentalism an ideology? An issue? A moral crusade? A science? A conspiracy aimed at the American way of life? There is no question that environmentalism is a powerful political movement. But there *is* some question as to whether it should be labeled an ideology. More particularly, some might argue that it should be considered simply an issue of concern to ideologues of a wide variety of persuasions; in other words, to the degree that it has ideological overtones, it is a part of other ideologies. For example, most modern reform liberals would argue that environmentalism is a part of their ideology. Reform liberals' concern for the environment is evident in their attempts to reduce or eliminate pollution through regulation of industry. Likewise, many socialists might claim that environmentalism is a component of socialism, arguing that the chief cause of environmental degradation is the capitalist's lust for private profit at the expense of the environment. Today even most conservatives, in the United States and elsewhere, claim to be "green."

Most environmentalists would reject each of these claims. American liberals and conservatives have argued about the speed and scope of their regulatory efforts, but they have always implicitly agreed on the primacy of capitalism, economic growth, and individual freedom. Concern for the environment takes a back seat to these ideological goals. The Eastern European and Soviet socialists have also proven that capitalists have no monopoly on pollution and environmental destruction. Their environment was sacrificed to the greater goal of fulfilling economic plans and competition with the West during the cold war. Eastern Europe is now littered with radioactive waste, toxic dumps, and deforested wastelands.

Environmentalists argue that both capitalism and socialism place economic production and growth above the environment. Although capitalists' and socialists' methods differ, they hold the same goal: human rationalization and mastery of the natural world, which they believe results in material wealth and comfort. Even in the traditional societies of the least economically developed countries, which cannot be realistically called capitalist or socialist, environmental decay is a terrible problem. Although they do not produce as much pollution or consume as many natural resources as do the economically developed countries, they generally view environmentalism as an unaffordable luxury. Unfortunately, feeding their people and developing their economies in the short term often results in the long-term destruction of their environment.

Therefore, in the opinion of environmentalists, no other popular ideology anywhere in the world truly addresses their values. Perhaps environmentalists are justified in claiming they constitute a separate and independent ideological movement. At a minimum, all other ideologies fall short of environmentalists' requirements. Chapter 1 outlines the functions of ideology; namely, ideology provides ethical standards, predictive theory, historical explanation, ideals and goals, methods and solutions, a call to action, group identification, and (negatively) propaganda and manipulation. Environmentalism does seem to meet this standard definition of an ideology.

THE EMERGENCE OF ENVIRONMENTALISM

It could be argued that modern environmentalism actually represents a return to a more ancient ideological value. Ancient humans lived in much closer contact with the natural world and in some ways understood its subtleties and nuances better than do modern humans. Of course, modern science has allowed us to catalogue and describe nature to an unprecedented degree. However, as technology proceeds, humans become more and more isolated individually from the natural world. In fact, this result is a fairly good definition of the word *progress*: victory over the forces of nature. To modern humans, progress means good health, the guarantee of food and shelter, labor-saving inventions, comfort and leisure, and so on. Few environmentalists advocate a true return to nature—without technological progress, humans are threatened by the natural forces of disease, famine, bad weather, discomfort, and deprivation. However, the inevitable result of our progress is that we lose contact with our natural environment and become creatures of technology instead.

Although environmentalism can be described as an emerging ideology, concern for the environment, or ecosphere, is definitely not a new issue. Thomas Malthus warned in *An Essay on the Principle of Population* (1798) that the earth's population was growing faster than were the available resources to feed and provide for it. Malthus originally argued that the inevitable result of this principle was war, famine, and disease, each of which temporarily reduces population levels until the crisis reemerges yet again. Later, Malthus argued that population growth could be restrained to prevent such catastrophes, although this was difficult to achieve and therefore unlikely to occur. Such pessimism about human achievement was rare and controversial in Malthus's time; classical liberals, classical conservatives, and classical socialists all believed in the inevitable subjugation or conquering of nature for the betterment of humanity.

Liberals, conservatives, and socialists also spoke of the creation of value, or wealth, out of land through the addition of labor. As such, they recognized no intrinsic value of land itself, other than its potential for exploitation through human labor and "development." Even today, local tax authorities refer to property development as the "improvement" of land.

> "This we know—the earth does not belong to man; man belongs to the earth. All things are connected like the blood that unites us all. Man did not weave the web of life—he is merely a strand in it. Whatever he does to the web, he does to himself."
>
> —Chief Seattle (1852)

To Native Americans, and to other more traditional nations around the world, the idea of owning and exploiting the earth is profoundly confusing. To the Cree Nation, who are witnessing the methyl mercury contamination of James Bay (Canada) and the destruction of its contributory rivers owing to the construction of hydroelectric dams, the term *land improvement* is insultingly misleading. The native people of the Brazilian rainforests feel likewise; they are almost helpless in their fight against the rape of the rainforests for short-term farming and mining profits. Whether they are located in the Pacific Islands or central Africa, members of nontechnological societies agree: humans cannot separate themselves from nature without risking their survival as a species. Modern American Indian leaders, such as Russel Means, speak of rationalism as "a curse" because it removes humans from the natural world. For Means, European ideology and science have stripped nature of its complexity and spirituality, thereby justifying its destruction in the name of ever-greater material wealth. Although this is certainly a frontal assault on classical liberalism and classical socialism, it is quite consistent with the classical conservatives' irrationalism.

In the United States, environmentalism can be traced to the conservation and preservation movements of the early 1900s. The **conservationists** fought to preserve land as national parks and wildlife refuges, and to control water usage. They stressed the responsible use and management of natural resources. These resources should be exploited, they claimed, but not wasted or spoiled. The unofficial leader of the conservation movement was President Theodore Roosevelt, who by 1908 quadrupled the acreage of forests in government preserves. The moderate proposals of the conservationists were often challenged by the more radical campaign of the **preservationists**, such as the Sierra Club (founded in 1892) and the Audubon Society, who considered the conservationists far too willing to put the environment at risk. The preservationists were unwilling to tolerate any substantial environmental damage caused by economic growth, especially in the virgin lands of the

West. The conservationists' position was somewhere between that of the preservationists and the Western land developers.

THE MODERN ENVIRONMENTAL MOVEMENT

The second phase of environmentalism began in the 1960s and quickly became a worldwide movement. The spark that set it in motion may have been the publication of Rachel Carson's *Silent Spring* in 1962, in which she warned of the long-term dangers of **pollution**, especially pesticides such as DDT. In addition to the danger posed by pesticides, environmentalists warned the world of radioactive and toxic wastes, ocean dumping of garbage, oil and chemical spills, smog-causing emissions, the salinization of rivers, topsoil erosion, chemical fertilizer runoff, the greenhouse effect, ozone depletion, acid rain, and the like. A variety of other organizations have since been formed, such as the Environmental Defense Fund, Friends of the Earth, Greenpeace, the Natural Resources Defense Council, the Nature Conservancy, the Wilderness Society, the World Wildlife Fund, and the Worldwatch Institute. In 1969 the United States enacted the National Environmental Policy Act, which requires an environmental impact statement for major federal construction or engineering projects. The Environmental Protection Agency (EPA) was founded in 1970, as was the first Earth Day.

Modern environmentalists have identified a number of threats other than the results of pollution. A second concern is **overpopulation**, which results in famine and disease. As of September 1996, the world population was approximately 5.85 billion and was growing at a rate of three per second, or 95 million per year. Experts disagree whether current agricultural production is adequate to meet the population's demand. Although the earth is capable of producing sufficient calories to feed the entire population, transportation problems make it difficult to distribute the food where it is needed. Alternatively, the production of food can be relocated to areas of greater need. However, even if these obstacles can be overcome, there does exist an inevitable limit to population growth. Whether through mass starvation and fatal illnesses, or through zero population growth (ZPG), the earth's population will eventually stabilize. A 1978 U.S. State Department study estimated that if by 1980 the average world couple limited their child-bearing to slightly more than two children (replacement-level fertility), world population would stabilize at about 6.4 billion.*
That has not happened. The same study calculated that if replacement-

---

* *Source:* U.S. Department of State, "World Population: The Silent Explosion—Part I, *Department of State Bulletin* 78 (October 1978): p. 50.

level fertility was not reached until 2000, the world population would reach about 8 billion by 2050 and would eventually stabilize at 8.4 billion. If this goal is not reached until 2040 instead, we can expect a population of about 14.5 billion by 2070, stabilizing at 15.1 billion. Recent United Nations studies project Earth's population to stabilize shortly after the year 2100 at between 10 and 20 billion, with the most likely result being about 12 billion.* Many recent demographers believe that the earth cannot sustain more than 10 billion in any case.

Famine is the most obvious result of overpopulation, but it should be noted that population growth also causes additional production and, therefore, additional pollution and resource depletion. Thus each of these problems is interrelated. Even if food could be produced in sufficient quantities to supply 15 billion people, what would this do to the earth's mineral and fuel resources, which are already threatened with depletion by 5 billion? How much additional pollution and ecological damage would occur?

The destruction of delicate ecosystems, a process sometimes called **ecocide**, is a third threat. In their attempts to "improve" on nature (to improve agricultural harvests, control a pest, beautify an area, etc.), humans have introduced plants and animals into new environments. The placement of alien species into natural ecosystems results in unexpected consequences. The complex relationships between the various members of an ecosystem develop slowly over thousands of years; when new species are introduced, they typically upset the balances between other members. Quite often this leads to the unchecked dominance of one or several species, which in turn leads to a general breakdown of the ecosystem. This and other kinds of human tampering threaten ecosystems, which in turn threatens the entire ecosphere.

Human activity has also caused the extinction of a wide variety of species, resulting in less biological diversity and the permanent loss of genetic stocks and potential variability. Although individual species extinction is a naturally occurring (but slow and rare) phenomenon, human manipulation of nature has exponentially accelerated the process.

A fourth global environmental threat is **nonrenewable resource depletion**. Although most people are aware of the ongoing depletion of fossil fuels, they are less aware of the diminishing supplies of metals and minerals. The first law of thermodynamics is the conservation of energy, which suggests that the measure of energy in the universe is constant and cannot be created or destroyed, although it can be transferred from one form to another. The second law of thermodynamics explains **entropy**: the *use* of energy transfers it into a different form, dissipating it and mak-

* *Source:* World Population Projection: Two Centuries of Population Growth, 1950–2150 (New York: United Nations, 1992).

ing it less "available" for later use. For example, available energy, in the form of water in the mountains, can be used as it descends through a hydroelectric dam to generate electricity, but once it reaches the bottom this energy is no longer available. It then requires work from other available energy sources (e.g., the sun) to be recycled (by evaporating and raining into the mountains again).

If all our machines were powered directly by the sun, we would not have much of a problem. However, we rely heavily on concentrated solar power—fossil fuels, which are nonrenewable. Fossil fuels dissipate available energy into heat (most of which is lost into space) and pollution (which represents unavailable energy). Although entropy is a natural process, technology has accelerated it. Humans are dissipating energy far faster than the sun's available energy can be concentrated into a useable form and faster than the sun can transfer (recycle) energy back into a useable form. *Equilibrium* will eventually be reached, in which there is no more available energy in the system (Earth). This is called *heat death*. Of course, the sun is also experiencing entropy, although we can continue to depend on it for several billion years.

Humans are also dissipating metals and minerals, making them unavailable for future use; only about a third are now being recycled. As for recycling, it requires making large amounts of energy unavailable to make dissipated metals "available" again—which still increases entropy of the system. Sunlight alone cannot stop the entropy of the earth—erosion of the topsoil, dispersion of metals and minerals into unavailable forms, and so on. For example, metal ore is mined, concentrated further, and then used, slowly dispersing it into the environment and into unreclaimable amounts. Every time metal strikes metal, the friction disperses molecules of the metal into the air, soil, or water. The more human activity, the greater is the process of entropy.

On a broader scale, the law of entropy holds that order tends toward disorder over time. In the state of equilibrium, not only would all energy be unavailable but matter would be dispersed into worthless uniformity. This is called *matter chaos*.

A fifth global environmental threat is the rapid growth of **dangerous technologies**. Even though science may be the answer to many global problems, its also the cause of those same problems. For example, although advances in medical technology and nutrition have saved lives, the consequent greater population growth has further taxed the earth's resources. Genetic engineering offers great hope but also has the potential to create a nightmarish assault on ecosystems. Our attempt to enhance national security through technology has also given us nuclear, biological, and chemical weapons, which in turn threaten us as well. For that matter, they threaten the survival of the human species itself.

"Mankind must put an end to war, or war will put an end to mankind."
—John F. Kennedy (1961)

The Limits to Growth (1972), published by an international group of environmentalists calling themselves the Club of Rome, was perhaps the most shocking description of the problem facing the ecosphere. Through the use of computer modeling of worldwide population growth, agricultural production, industrial production, pollution, and use of nonrenewable resources, the Club of Rome set about calculating the future of the earth. They concluded that the earth was approaching a global catastrophic crash of the ecosphere and its human inhabitants, within a century. Even when the model was adjusted to allow for the most optimistic possible circumstances, it still forecast doom. Since the publication of *The Limits to Growth* there has been a great debate about the Club of Rome's methodology (its mathematical formulas, the assumptions of the model, etc.), but few environmentalists doubt its basic message of warning, and evidence continues to mount of the danger posed by the rapid growth of population and industrial production.

Environmentalists conclude that any possible solution to this predicament must be immediate, comprehensive, and global. *Immediacy* is required because the slide into catastrophe may be sudden and impossible to avert, once it begins. The solution must be *comprehensive* in the sense that it must address all the global problems together, because each is interdependent. (For example, population control in the poorer countries will accelerate their economic development and increase their standard of living, thereby boosting their use of resources and creation of pollution.) Finally, any solution must be *global*—environmentalists are necessarily internationalists, because individual countries cannot solve the problem alone. Countries that insist on their sovereign right to act without international regulation, and that do not cooperate in fighting these problems, will ruin the environment for all. Most environmentalists believe the United Nations must assume a greater role in regulating the ecosphere and world peace because these are "public goods," that is, they are commonly shared by all nations of the world. One of the most influential books to make this point was Lester Brown's *World Without Borders* (1972), which he dedicated to "a world order in which conflict and competition among nations will be replaced with cooperation and a sense of community." The international movement for environmentalism may be most noticeable in the growing electoral power of political parties called the **Greens**, especially in Europe, and in the internationalization of various interest groups such as Greenpeace, the Worldwatch Institute, and the World Wildlife Fund.

Voters and the Environment

"This country should do whatever it takes to protect the environment."
   Agree Strongly = 65%   Agree, Not Strongly = 12%   Total = 77%

"This country has gone too far in its efforts to protect the environment."
   Agree Strongly = 13%   Agree, Not Strongly = 7%   Total = 20%

"Stricter environmental laws and regulations are worth the cost."
   Agree Strongly = 47%   Agree, Not Strongly = 14%   Total = 61%

"Stricter environmental laws and regulations cost too many jobs and hurt the economy."
   Agree Strongly = 23%   Agree, Not Strongly = 12%   Total = 35%

Source: "Voter Anxiety Dividing GOP; Energized Democrats Backing Clinton," *Times Mirror Center for the People and the Press,* November 14, 1995, p. 96.

RADICAL ENVIRONMENTALISM

There exists at least as much division among environmentalists as there is among conservatives, liberals, Marxists, or other ideologues. The mainstream of the movement is challenged today by a radical environmentalism, sometimes called the **third wave** of environmentalism. Consensus is relatively easy to build when costs and inconveniences of environmental protection are minor and perceived benefits are great. However, nonenvironmentalists are increasingly suspicious of environmentalism and are increasingly questioning the growing costs. For example, the cleanup of toxic waste sites in the United States currently costs about $10 billion per year. Unfortunately for environmentalists, the benefits of environmental controls are often intangible or otherwise hard to identify in strict dollar amounts, although in many cases they may vastly outweigh the costs. For example, in a report released in June 1996 the Environmental Protection Agency (EPA) estimated that although enforcement of the Clean Air Act cost businesses and consumers $20 billion in 1990, it saved at least $400 billion in saved health-care costs, lost workdays, reduced productivity, and other problems associated with air pollution.* However, most Americans do not consciously consider the long-term savings derived from environmental protection, and opponents will undoubtedly ques-

* *Source:* "Clean Air Act Payoff," *Houston Chronicle,* June 11, 1996, p. 9a.

tion the reliability of the EPA's findings. For this reason, most environmentalists have been careful not to push too hard for rapid changes in public attitude and behavior, fearing a backlash.

Radical environmentalists are unwilling to make compromises. They insist on nothing less than a complete restructuring of the world's social, political, and economic way of life. They include organizations such as the Sea Shepherd Society and Earth First!, which have employed sabotage (what they call **ecotage**) to wreck fishing vessels, bulldozers, drilling and mining equipment, company offices, and the like. An organization named the Animal Liberation Front has freed animals from zoos and research laboratories. Earth First! became well known for its "tree spiking": driving large nails into a sample of a forest's trees and labeling the forest *spiked* so that lumbermen would not risk hitting the nails and ruining their power saws and injuring or killing themselves. Opponents have labeled this **ecoterrorism**.

Most radical environmentalists call themselves **deep ecologists**. By *deep* they imply that their views are more serious than those of "weekend environmentalists" who do not practice what they preach. Being deep means fundamentally altering one's behavior in purchasing products, shunning un-Green activities, conserving and recycling resources, contributing money, and becoming a political activist if not a revolutionary. Deep ecologists accuse the mainstream environmental movement of **anthropocentrism** (human-centeredness, implying the assumed superiority of human life and the exclusion of nonhuman life from ethical and moral questions). Deep ecologists are not in disagreement with the Enlightenment's dignification of individual human life, but they want to expand it to include other forms of life and to balance it with human responsibility to be a good steward of nature. The mindset that puts human interests above all others is arrogant, they argue.

Even among radical environmentalists themselves, however, there is a variety of purpose. Some are primarily **animal rights** advocates who believe humans have no fundamental right to deny life, liberty, and the pursuit of happiness to animals. At least, they say, humans have an obligation to avoid causing unnecessary suffering by animals.

Others, such as **social greens** (also called *leftist greens* or *social ecologists*), are more humanistic and reject animal rights advocates and other deep ecologists who seemingly equate animal life with human life. Social greens focus on *social* (broadly including political and economic) organization and behavior and how that causes environmental problems. They argue that the key to environmental protection is the empowerment of average citizens at the grassroots level who will then naturally act to protect their urban environments, workplaces, homes, and countryside from degradation. Apathetic or powerless citizens cannot successfully resist the pollution of their environments by those who profit from it.

This requires democratizing and decentralizing government further and extending real political power to those who are less influential now—such as women, ethnic minorities, and the poor—to create what they call **environmental justice**. There does exist substantial evidence that environmental degradation occurs most frequently in poorer communities that are less politically activist.*

A subset of the social greens are the **ecofeminists**, who attribute the environmental crisis to male aggressiveness and domination that is transferred into human domination of the environment. Just as human freedom requires gender equality and liberation from stifling sex roles, they argue, it also requires liberation from traditional (male) ways of thinking about the control and exploitation of the environment.

One of the most radical philosophies is that of the **Gaians**. *Gaia*, or *Gaea*, is Greek for "earth"; Gaia was the goddess of Earth in ancient mythology. Gaians see the earth as a single living organism composed of humans, animals, plants, and inorganic substances. It adapts and evolves just as do other living things. Whereas environmentalists are generally most concerned about the ability of the biosphere to nourish human life, Gaians believe that the health of Earth (Gaia) is what matters most. Whether individual species live or die will inevitably come second to the survival of Gaia as a living and adapting organism. (Similarly, social insects like bees and ants act as if they were a single organism; individuals routinely commit suicidal "kamikaze" attacks, protecting their colony's [and thus their common genes'] survival and reproduction.)†
What is it that most threatens Gaia's delicate ecosphere? What one element acts as a cancer, damaging other constituent parts? What one species, if sacrificed, would allow Gaia to survive and even recover from its ecological disease? If the Gaians are correct, Gaia will protect itself through the extinction of humankind. This leads the Gaians to a fatalistic and pacifistic conclusion that humanity is doomed to destroy itself and that no amount of environmental activism can stop it.

THE SUSTAINABLE SOCIETY

The modern environmental movement is diverse and ideological. It includes the anti-humanistic Gaians at one end of the spectrum and the conservationists who simply want to conserve wildlife for continued hunting and exploitation at the other end of the spectrum. Neither group is typ-

---

* *Source:* See EcoNet's Environmental Racism/Environmental Justice Resources. Online. Internet. 2 September, 1996. Available http://www.igc.apc.org/envjustice/

† *Source:* Dawkins, Richard, *The Selfish Gene*. new edition (Oxford: Oxford University Press, 1989), p. 171–181.

ical of the whole. In the center is the mainstream of the movement, which wants to expand the classical conservatives' organic society to include not just the social community of humans but the biosphere in which we live. Their methods vary from scientific and technological approaches, to ethical persuasion, to the increased use of market incentives (such as the sale of pollution permits), to increased national and international government regulations. Their goal is the **sustainable society**: a society that can survive and prosper without destroying the ecosphere in the process.

Modern society's current insatiable desire for economic growth and material consumption carries a heavy environmental price and arguably has left humanity no happier or socially harmonious. As the title of Paul Wachtel's *The Poverty of Affluence* (1989) implies, consumerism and the accumulation of goods has left Western society impoverished—that is, psychologically depressed and spiritless, and without a sense of civil responsibility. By any objective measure of material wealth, Americans are becoming more and more wealthy and are increasingly surrounded by labor-saving devices and wondrous technologically advanced products. Yet at the same time social ills and discontent flourish, and the environment is threatened with collapse. Clearly the sustainable society requires a redefinition of the concepts of progress and prosperity. The sustainable society tolerates growth only if it occurs without a depletion of resources or environmentally harmful effects. It demands constant and careful stewardship of the ecosphere.

Key Terms

biosphere	Greens
ecosphere	third wave
ecosystems	ecotage, ecoterrorism
environmentalism	deep ecologists
conservationism	anthropocentrism
preservationism	animal rights
pollution	social greens
overpopulation	environmental justice
ecocide	ecofeminism
nonrenewable resource depletion	Gaians
entropy	sustainable society
dangerous technologies	

Study Questions

1. Is environmentalism an ideology? Why or why not?
2. In what way is environmentalism a challenge to the Enlightenment and to classical conservatism, classical liberalism, and classical socialism?

3. Is environmentalism ancient or modern?
4. How do the differences between the conservationists and the preservationists compare to the differences between modern mainstream environmentalists and radical environmentalists?
5. What dangers have modern environmentalists identified? What does it mean to say that these problems are interrelated?
6. According to environmentalists, what is required of any solution to the global environmental crisis?
7. Who are the radical environmentalists?
8. What are the similarities and differences between the classical conservatives' and the environmentalists' concepts of organicism and irrationalism?
9. What does the term *progress* mean? Why must this concept be reevaluated, according to environmentalists?
10. Do environmentalists offer any alternative to an impending environmental collapse?

CHAPTER 11

THE FUTURE OF IDEOLOGY

TRENDS

What ideological trends are most evident in the world today? The most obvious is the decline of authoritarianism around the globe. Whereas a half-century ago pluralism was uncommon, the majority of countries today have constitutional, multiparty, republican forms of government with free elections and freedom of the press, although in varying degrees. Pluralism is increasingly the standard by which the world community judges the political legitimacy (but not the basic sovereignty) of its members. Although most countries of the world are still far from the democratic ideal, few authoritarian governments have been unchanged by at least moderate reform in the last decade.

The decline of authoritarianism goes hand in hand with the growth of internationalism and the apparent renewal of capitalism. As the world capitalist marketplace grows, and as the information age blossoms, it is increasingly difficult for authoritarians to isolate their political structures from outside influences. For example, Soviet social scientists convinced Gorbachev that future Soviet economic progress (not to mention military technological competitiveness) would require world trade and communication. It was impossible for Soviet scientists and economic planners to be innovative and up-to-date when they were limited in their contacts with foreigners and even each other, because of their authoritarian government's fear of open communication and dialogue. Cutting-edge technological progress is incompatible with a government that controls access to photocopiers and computer modems. Furthermore, the failures of the Soviets' rigid central planning have led to a renewed interest in the laissez-faire principles of Adam Smith.

However, two provisos must be inserted at this point. First, although it is true that internationalism is growing in a variety of ways, nationalism still reigns as probably the most important ideological force in the modern world. In fact, the end of the cold war has allowed a rebirth of nationalism in some regions, most notably Eastern Europe and the former Soviet Union. In the case of the former Yugoslavia, a virulent nationalism plunged the Serbs, Croats, and Muslims into an orgy of killing. In the United States as well as in most countries, the debate continues between internationalists and nationalists about the proper foreign policy role for the United States in the New World Order. And in many countries, fascism seems to be recruiting new followers.

Second, although authoritarian socialism has been largely discredited, socialism has not been rejected in relatively pluralistic countries such as those in Western Europe and elsewhere. In fact, socialism remains a partner to capitalism in many countries, resulting in mixed economies. And those who think that laissez-faire economics (or even the modern version of regulated capitalism) is now unchallenged should be reminded of the debate raging over corporatism.

THE END OF IDEOLOGY?

Finally, the disintegration of the Soviet Union has led some to say that ideology is dead. It is certainly true that the cold war ideological confrontation is greatly diminished. Francis Fukuyama, in *The End of History and the Last Man* (1992), argues that Western liberalism—with its capitalism, republicanism, pluralism, and libertarianism—is being accepted around the world as the superior ideology. In this view the world is reaching the end of its ideological evolution, and classical liberalism has triumphed. Fukuyama's thesis has triggered a debate concerning **endism**. However, this is not the first such debate. For example, Daniel Bell and other authors stirred a similar controversy in *The End of Ideology* (1962).

"Where there is no vision, the people perish."
—The Bible, Proverbs 29:18

Endism is, in my own opinion, highly myopic. Governments may come and go, but the fundamental debates continue. In fact, there are those who call for a comprehensive revision in the dominant ideological foundations of Western society. Most important, environmentalists have questioned whether humanity can survive with our present ideological values. They argue that neither capitalism nor socialism, each with a vision of human progress expressed in subduing and transforming nature, addresses the most severe of our problems—the destruction of the ecosphere. They argue that in an age of nuclear weapons, biogenetic engineering, and other dangerous technologies, nationalism is a prescription for disaster. They argue that unless humanity can adopt an environmentalist spirit and responsibly and communally manage the use of nature, all societies are doomed to failure. Ideology is *not* dead.

Key Term

endism

Study Questions

1. Which ideologies are growing in influence and which are declining? (Be careful not to exaggerate or overlook subtleties.)
2. Why do some say ideology is "dead"? What do they mean by this? Is it? Why or why not?